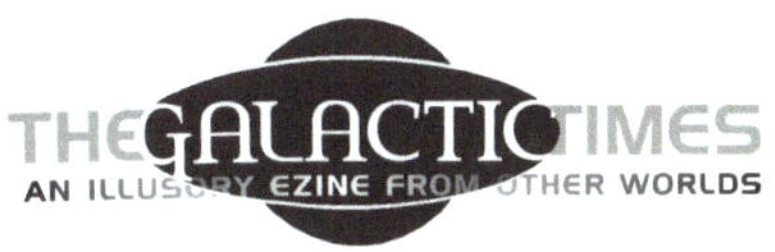

Tele-mail number: 9261
Thought Broadcast 13:28
Subscribe by winking at the Sun

Creatrix
(Visionary Speaking Tube)
Electric Serpent/Stephanie South
(a.k.a. Red Queen)

Cover art
Votan/Spectral Monkey

Graphics
Votan/Red Queen

Graphic Art, Cover & Layout Design:
Rhythmic Dragon/Jacob Wyatt
Rhythmic Sun/Kelly Harding
Sunshine Design

Interdimensional Telepathic Contributors
Starling Questward
Azakre Goldenwire
E-PA
Dor Jar El
ALPHA and OMEGA
Orel Ka (OK)
JJ and the Planetary Yogis
and all the Galactic Maya

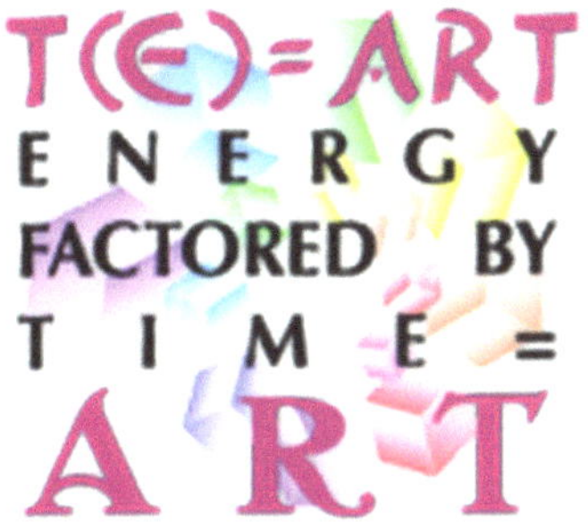

Contents

Regeneration through Imagination

Introduction

Welcome Interdimensional Shifters, Secret Dreamers and New Time Surfers to Volume One of **THE GALACTIC TIMES: AN ILLUSORY EZINE FROM OTHER WORLDS**. We received an S.O.S. signal from Planet Earth. Special emergency report. Collective morale is down.Humans need reminder that the HIGHEST DREAM IS REAL … YOU HOLD THE KEY. IMAGINATION DOES CHANGE THE WORLD!

We understand it has been quite a dark time on your planet. We have compassion. But we are here to remind you of Wonderful things. Do not lose heart now! A NEW FREQUENCY is being emitted from the galactic center. There is no past to return to.

Knowledge of the Law of Time is galactic medicine. Administer your medicine now! Become the Mystery of the Golden Ones! Untangle the star systems and find your Galactic family!

All knowledge has been made available to your planet. All are free to step out of the time distortion box. Do not compromise what you know. Do not underestimate the power that you have been given. If you have questions, please submit them to E-Pa.

The 13 Moon calendar is a passport into a rich mythic realm where secret gates are activated through Time codes. Memories are triggered as the synchronic highway opens to reveal the magical path of a regenerated timespace. Here can be entered a new mythic realm. Allow yourself to "Be nothing" then you will understand. See our cover story of Starling Questward's journey.

THE GALACTIC **TIMES** comes now as a reminder of your own power to re-imagine the world. Power is the invincible force from within that comes from following unswervingly a guiding vision. What is your vision? Because of your fluctuating amnesiac human tendencies we have given you daily practices to strengthen your memory and accelerate you toward the New Timespace.

A Bright new World awaits YOU. Saturate yourself in the New frequencies. Bathe in the light of the New Beam. Stay open to new perceptions. Activate forgotten knowledge. Repair your flux tube system, align it with the earth and vibrate into a rainbow. On the other side of the rainbow don't be surprised if you are greeted by the golden dolphin, the platinum hawk, the white-winged elephant and even the pink squirrel. Why not?

A Galactic Renaissance is at hand on your planet. Open the Churches of Imagination and sing the future hymns. What is your archetypal mythic story? What role will you play in the re-genesis of Timeship Earth?

Time Code: RQ185: TFI 1311: BMU 429. Kin 11.
*On Behalf of reunion of Twin Souls, Planets, Galaxies and Universes

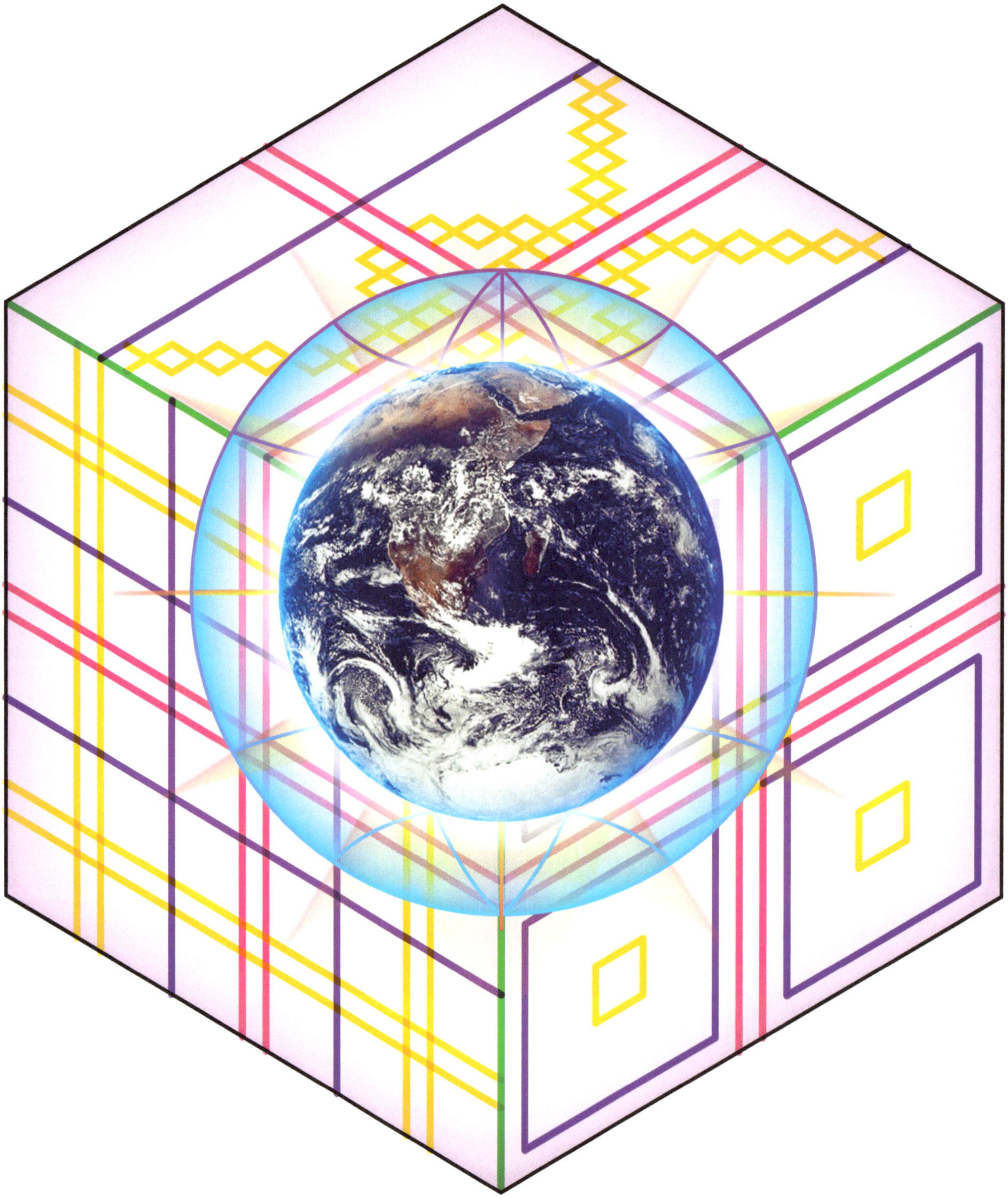

EARTH IS A TIMESHIP
PLANET HOLON

As you read these words you are traveling on a Timeship.

Planet Earth is a timespace hologram.

This timespace construct is coded into a vast cube matrix that is vibrating and pulsating mathematical structures from a radial matrix that connects everything to everything.

All of reality is a language of signs and symbols.

Everything that appears is a passing ephemeral manifestation,

and yet, it represents some different construct or value of another dimension.

By attuning your consciousness to the Earth, Sun and galactic beam, you will understand everything.

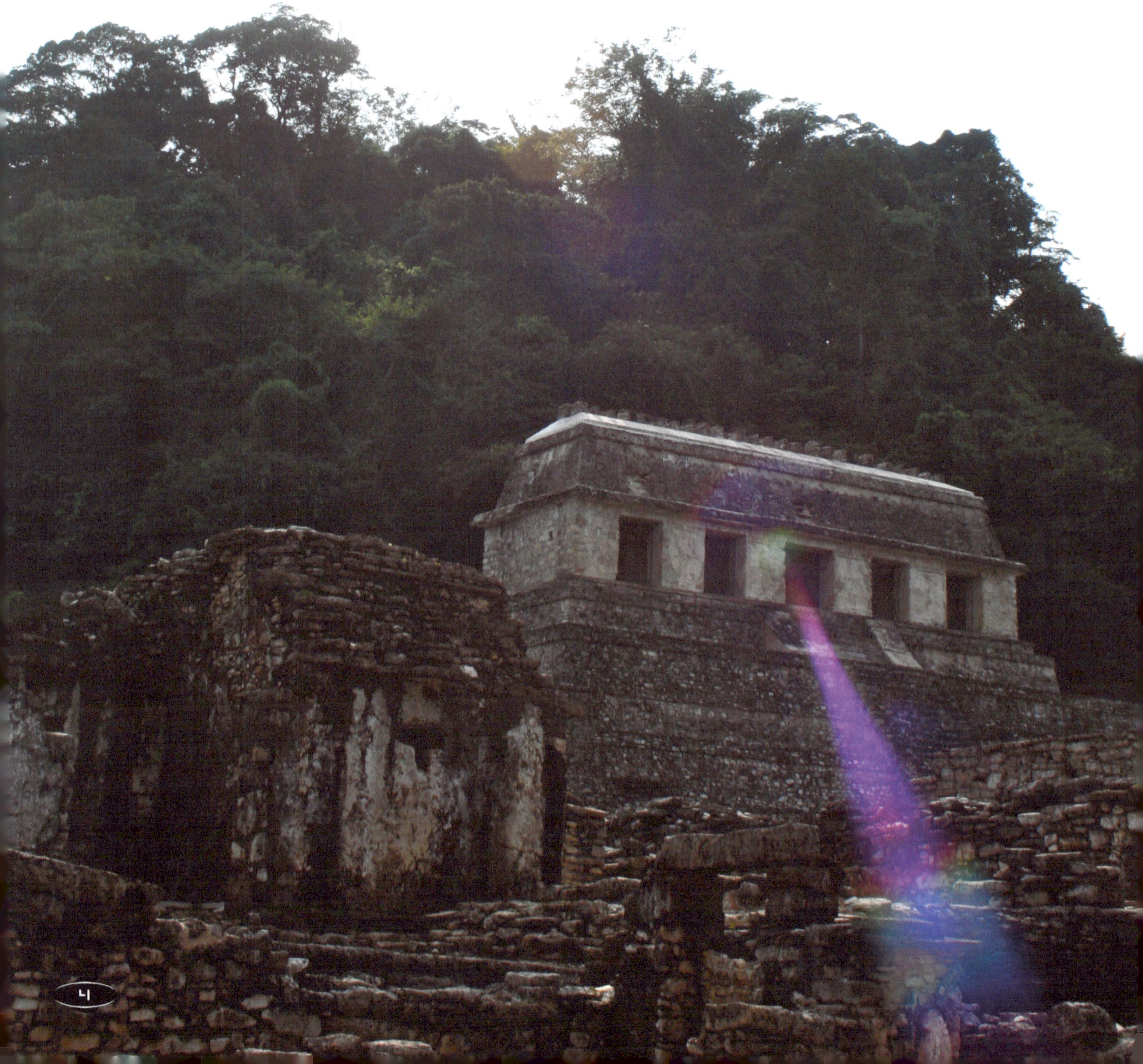

NEW GALACTIC BEAM TRANSMITS NEW FREQUENCY TO EARTH

I AM THE SOURCE OF LIGHT SUPREME — ENIGMATIC STOREHOUSE OF YOUR DEEPEST DREAM!

TOUCH ME WITH YOUR SOUL AND I WILL DISSOLVE AND MAKE YOU WHOLE!

The synchronic codes left by Pacal Votan are keys that unlock the secret passageway and activate the bridge that leads from this Earth to the New Earth.

This passageway brings us into relationship with the guiding intelligence of our Sun, Kinich Ahau.

But only those who discover their true essence will find the secret passageway.

The human being merely uses its
body apparatus

to tune into the consciousness or the mind
at large

from which it derives

thoughts, words and other forms of
communication.

Consciousness is not really the property of
the human being

nor is the question of intelligence.

BOOK OF THE THRONE: COSMIC HISTORY CHRONICLES VOL. I, P. 107

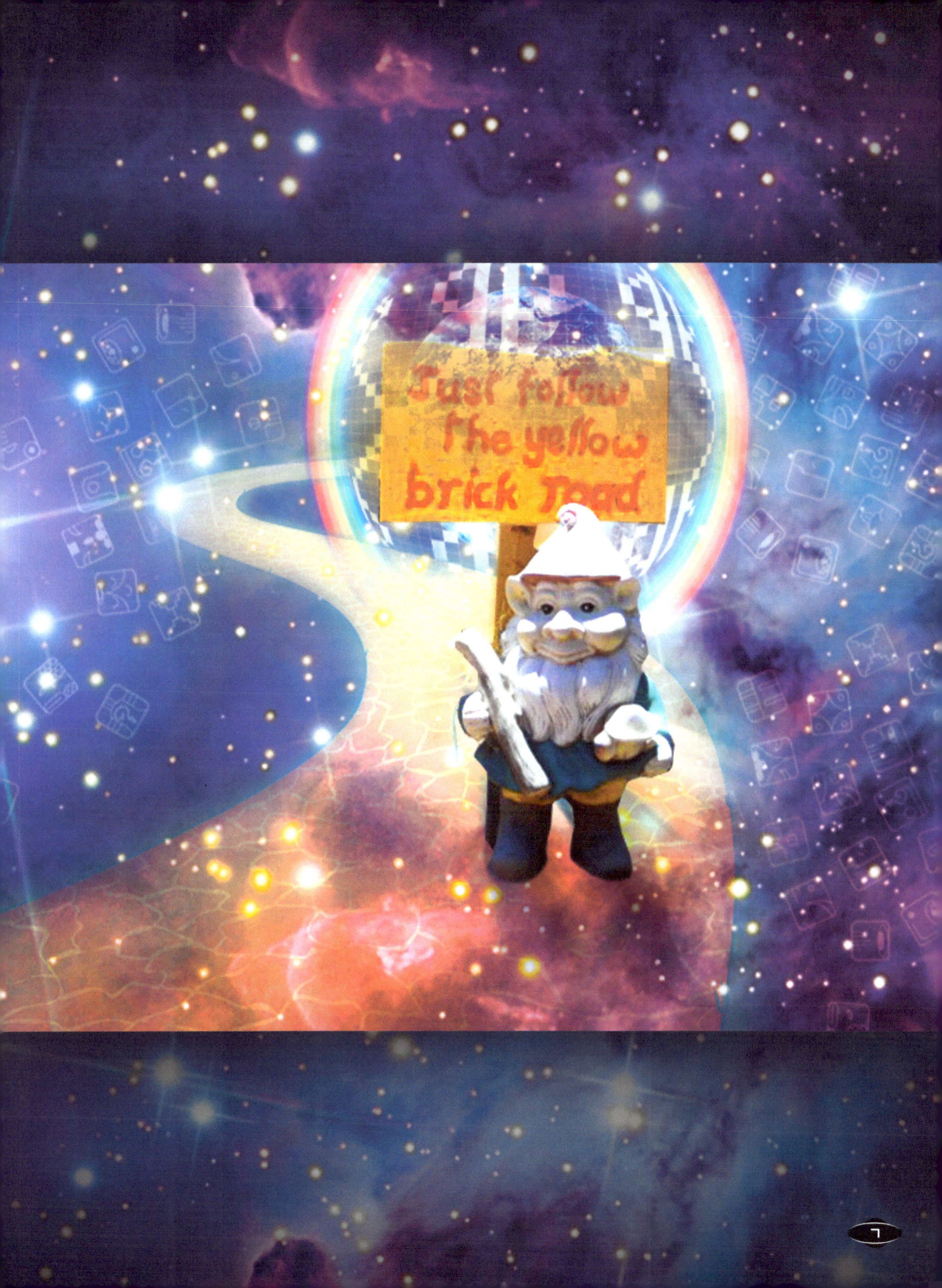
Just follow
the yellow
brick road

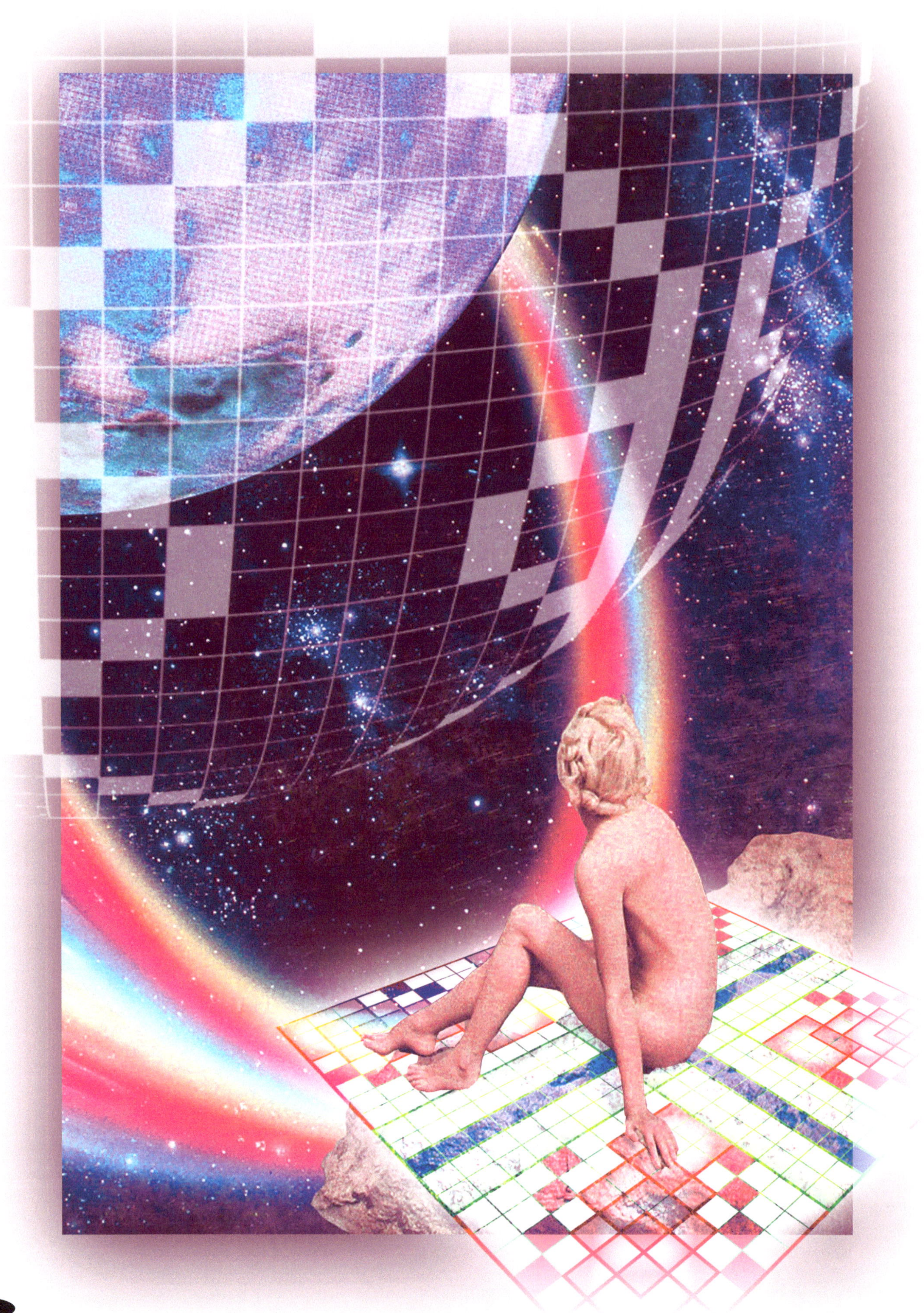

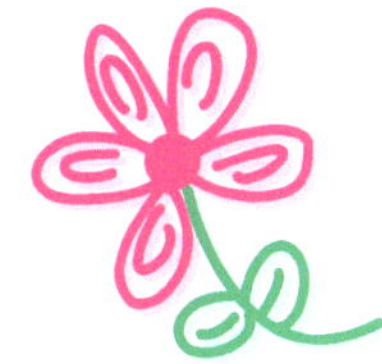

Dear Earth Lady,

To bloom – forget the image of them ~
their styles, their words, their lectures
their fears, their views, their gestures

LADY: But am I not that which I see?

Lady, once again – listen~
To bloom, forget the image of them–
their image, their thoughts–
        a Pandora's box!

LADY: But isn't that uncompassionate?
        and what do I have as a model to go by?

Lady wild – Go Forth!
        into the secret dream
        that pounds through pen & type
        own not the mind that runneth forth!
            Listen!
            Come stronger
            can you hear?
            unravel yourself!
            the truth is so near!
                of being "not them"
                    uninhibited!

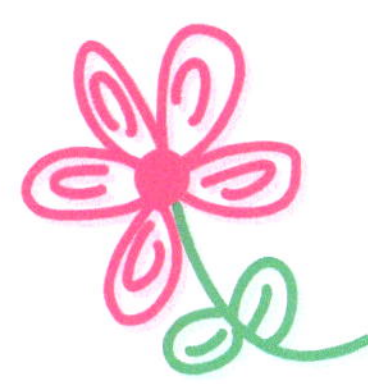

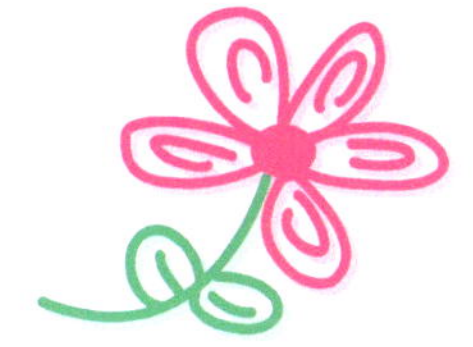

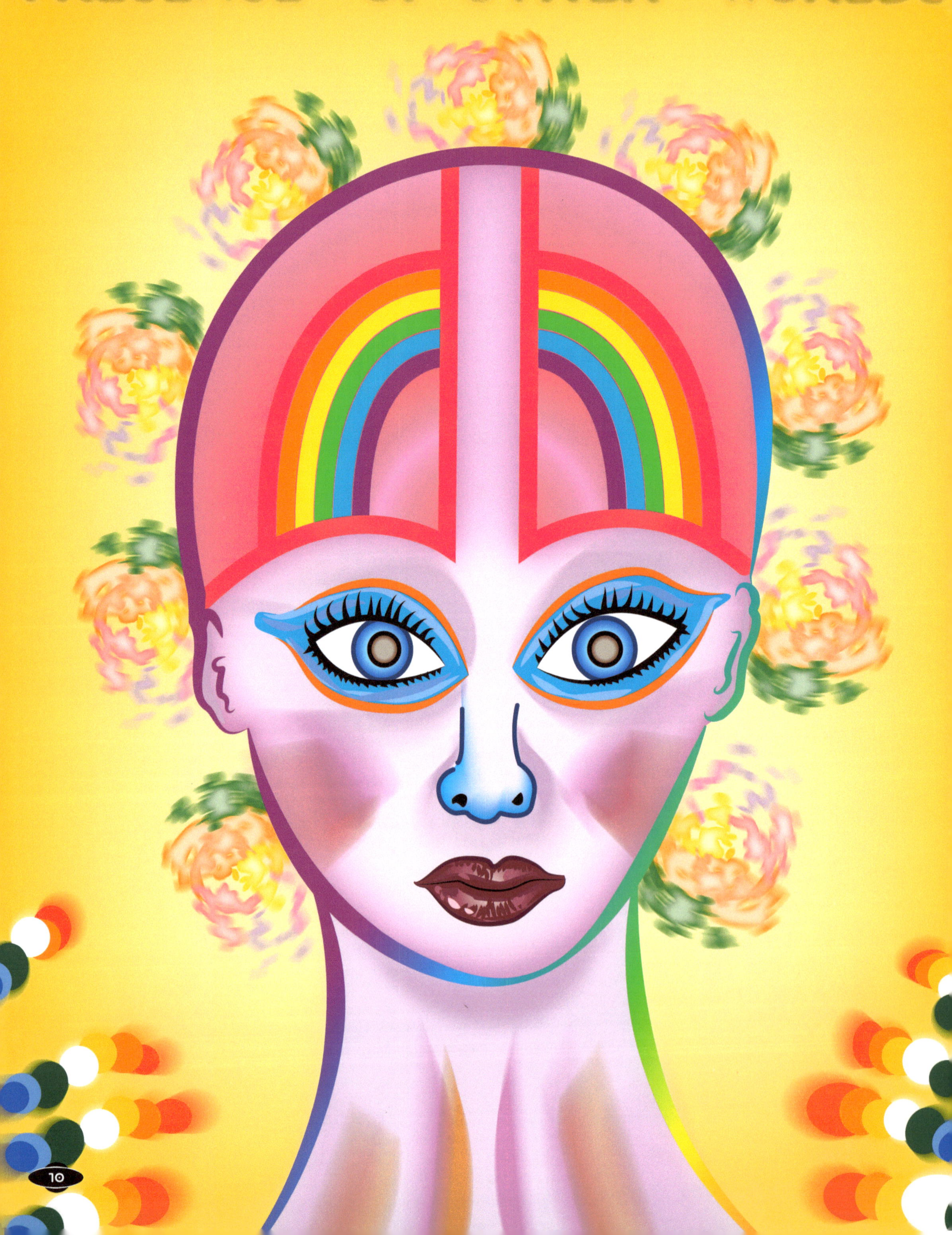

Higher evolved stellar systems and other galactic orders may investigate other lesser evolved systems through various advanced forms of time travel, but may not interfere in any way with the stream of consciousness until it has evolved into the point of moment to moment self-reflective consciousness. Only mutual telepathic awareness or recognition is allowed.

—DYNAMICS OF TIME, 2.9

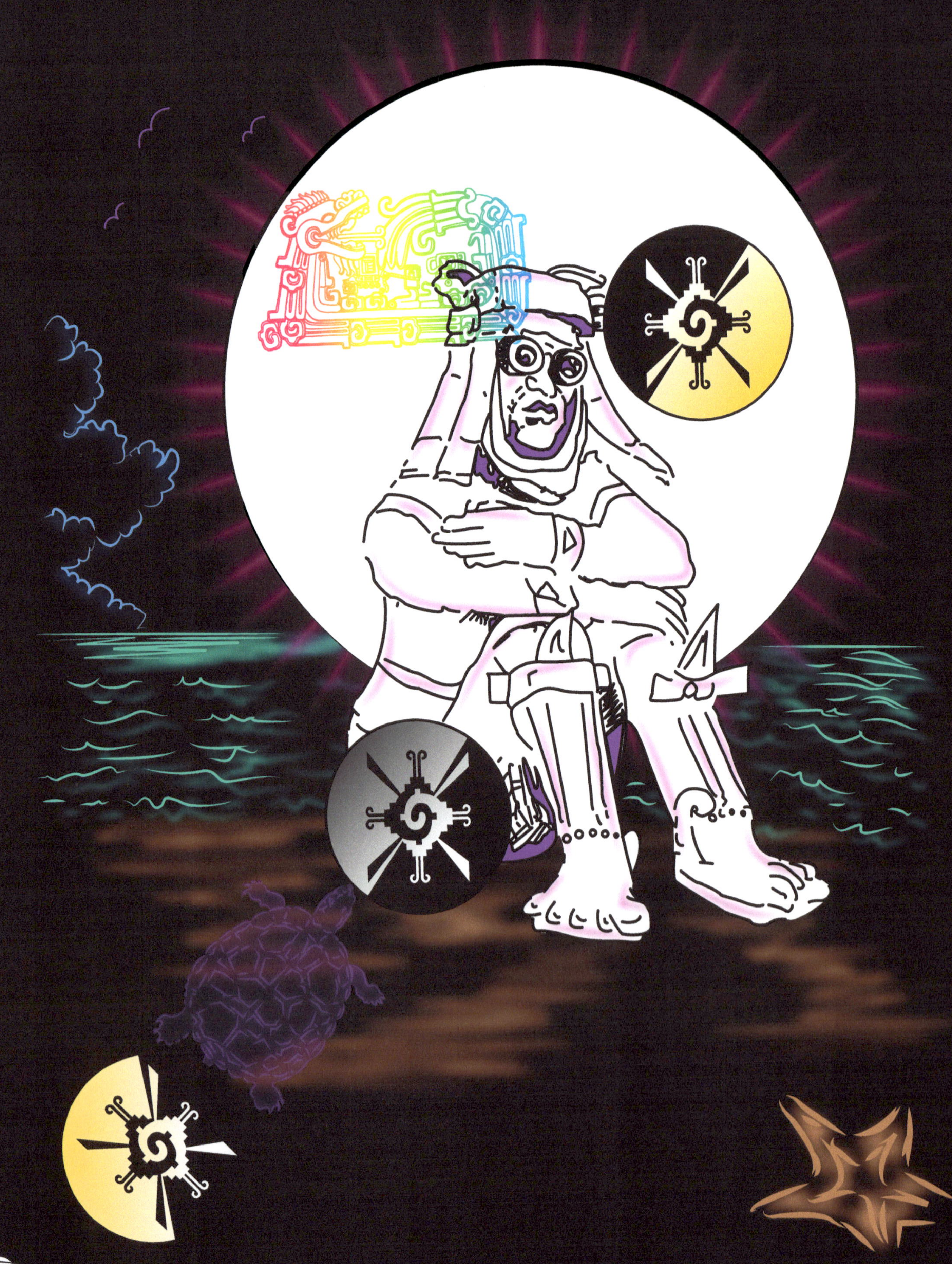

INTERDIMENSIONAL
INTERPLANETARY SOUL TRAVELER
VOTAN-SHAMANROCK

I'm an interdimensional interplanetary Soul Traveler
I been traveling a long ways to get to you
Yeah I said I'm an Interdimensional Interplanetary Soul Traveler
and I been traveling a long ways to get to you
You gotta stop living in the wrong time
You gotta go live in a time that's true

I landed all shipwrecked on one of your shores
Yeah, I landed all shipwrecked on one of your shores
it took a shaman to find and shake me to the core
Yeah it took that ancient shaman to shake me to the core

Hey here traveler, he said to me
Wake up and remember who you're supposed to be

Now I'm here as the messenger you need
Now I'm here as the messenger you need
I'm in your DNA, I'm your star seed

I've got the gift of second vision so I can tell what's wrong with you
I've got the gift of second vision so I can tell what's wrong with you
I'm here to change your calendar and give you something really new

chorus:
I'm an interdimensional interplanetary Soul Traveler
I been traveling a long ways to get to you
Yeah I said I'm an Interdimensional Interplanetary Soul Traveler
and I been traveling a long ways to get to you
You gotta stop living in the wrong time
You gotta go live in a time that's true

Thirteen moons it's not too late
Thirteen Moons its never out of date
Break free from the Babylonian man
Thirteen moons, its the Divine Plan

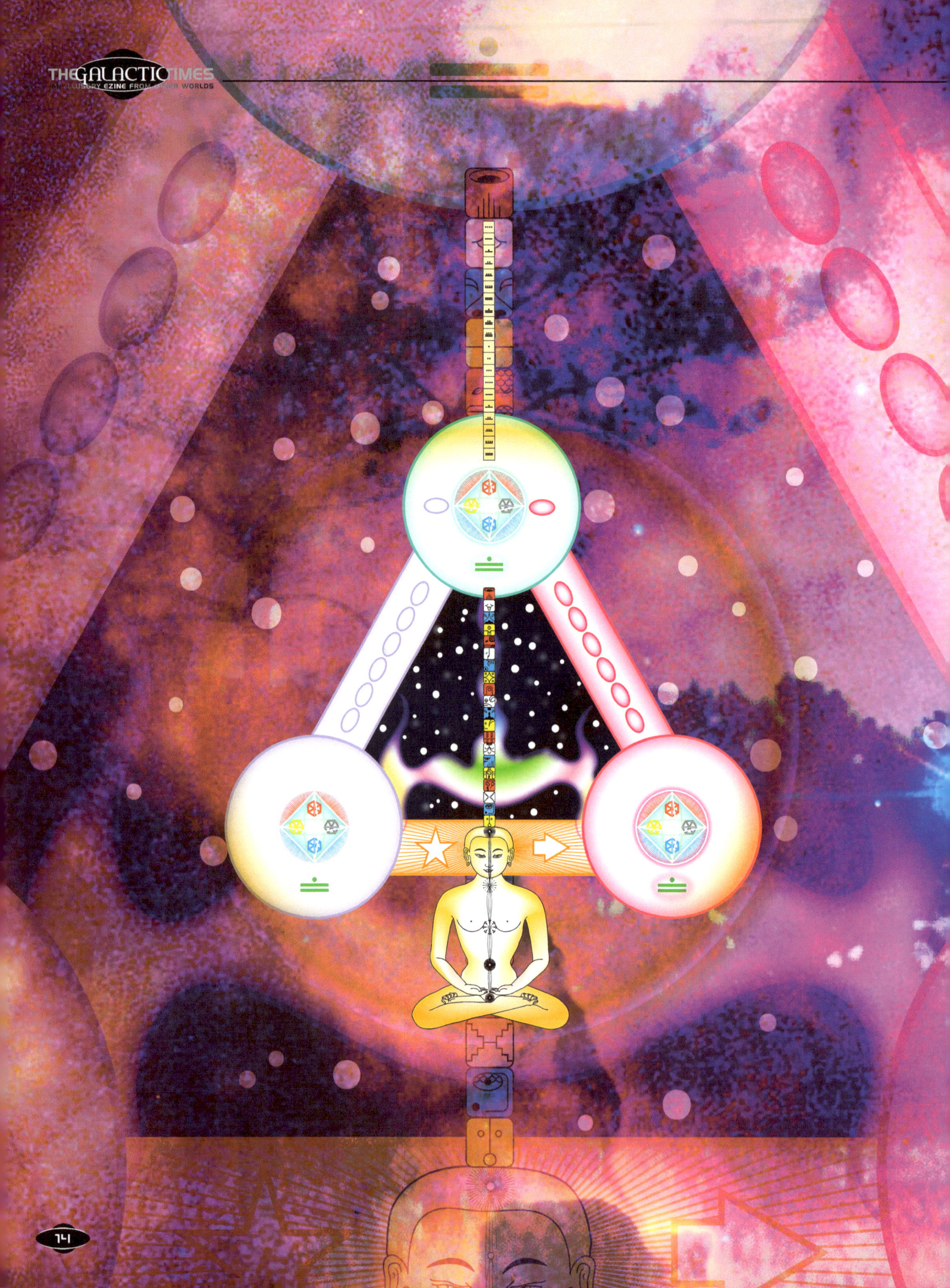

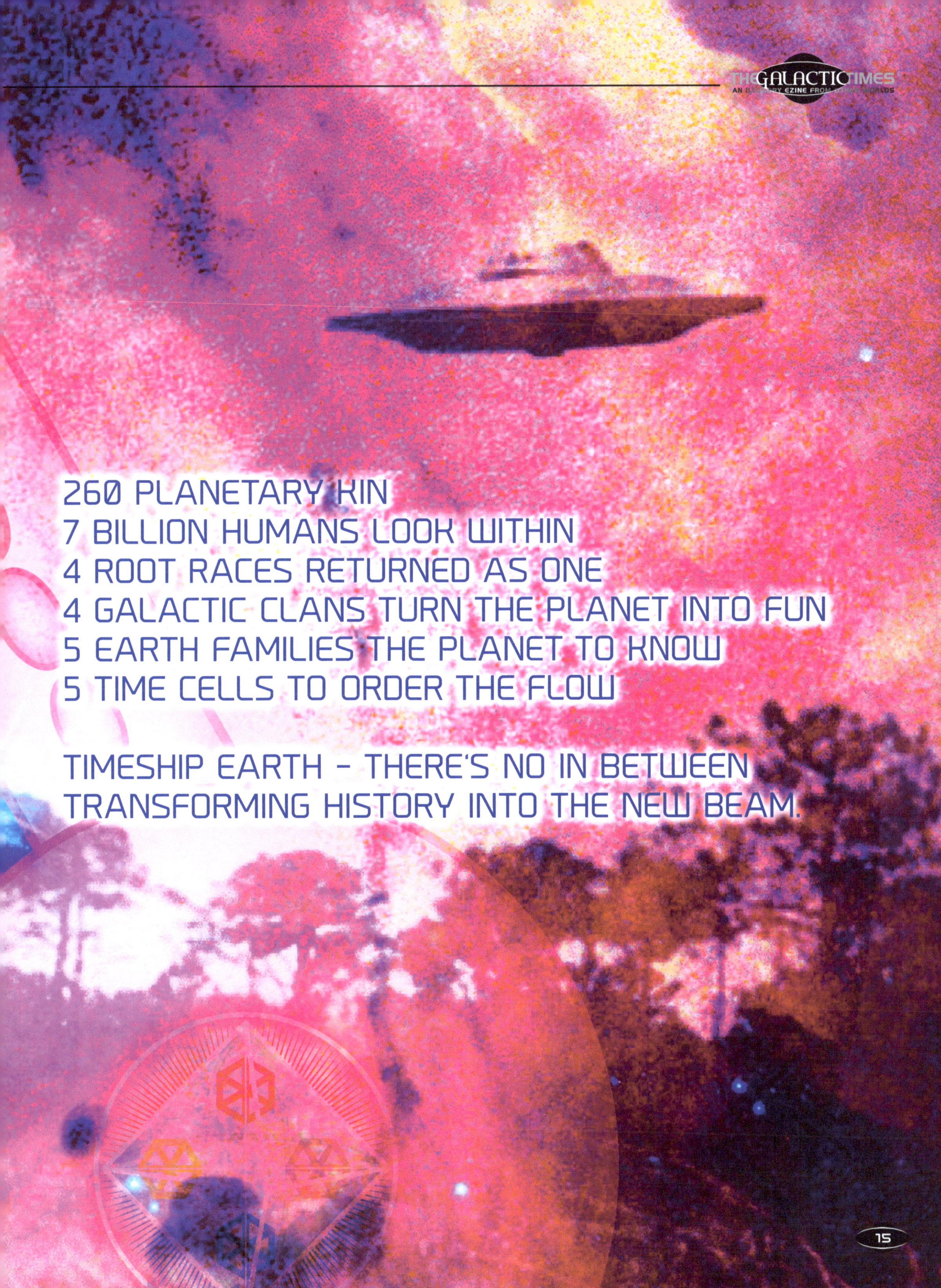

260 PLANETARY KIN
7 BILLION HUMANS LOOK WITHIN
4 ROOT RACES RETURNED AS ONE
4 GALACTIC CLANS TURN THE PLANET INTO FUN
5 EARTH FAMILIES THE PLANET TO KNOW
5 TIME CELLS TO ORDER THE FLOW

TIMESHIP EARTH – THERE'S NO IN BETWEEN
TRANSFORMING HISTORY INTO THE NEW BEAM.

I AM AZAKRE GOLDENWIRE

I bring a Reminder from Your Interdimensional Star Family.

There exist supermental civilizations, both within your home galaxy, and in parallel galaxies. We are your interdimensional family. We are constantly sending scanner beams to You.

Please open to Receive Us.

Though we speak of supermental civilizations in the plural, there is really only one super cosmic civilization. As you advance in telepathy, you will understand how space becomes the medium of unification of all minds.

Telepathy evolves a universal cosmic language—Irdin. The supermental civilizations represent a relative advance of intelligence in relationship to lesser evolved states contained in the Kar Dual galaxy types. Learn more about us in
Book of the Avatar: Cosmic History Chronicles, Volume 2.

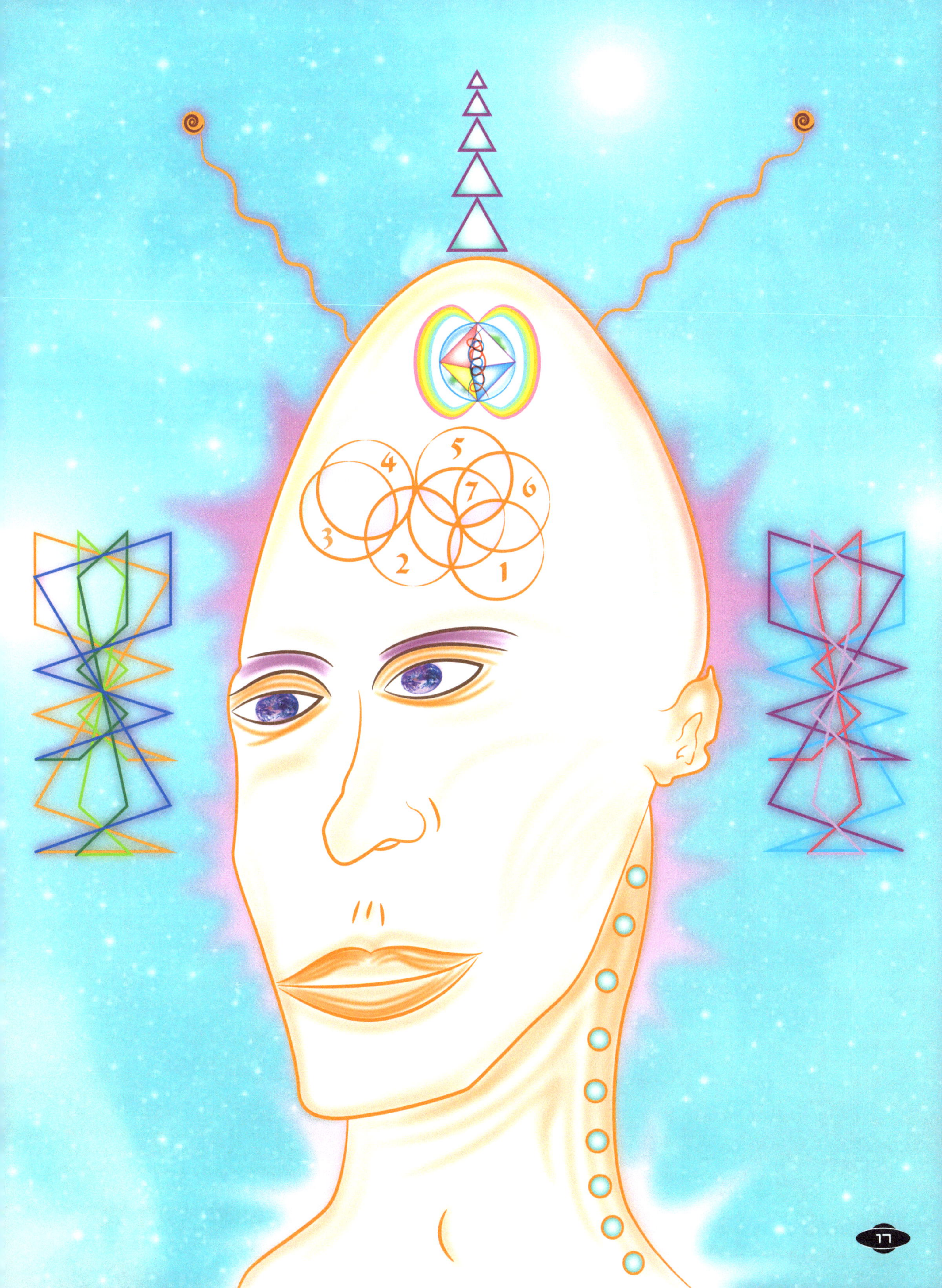

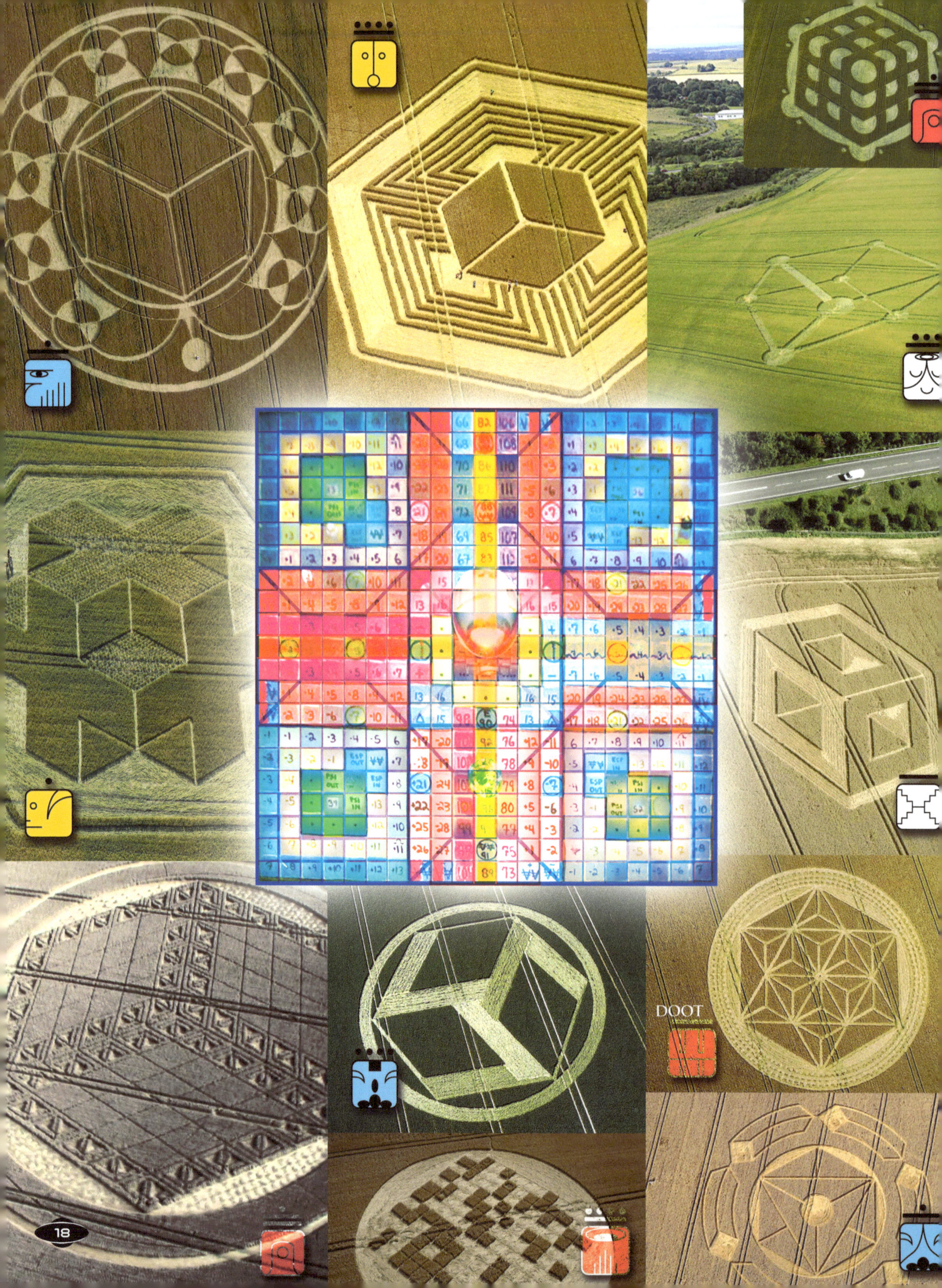

441

SYNCHRONIZATION IS ANTIDOTE TO MECHANIZATION

WELCOME TO THE PATH BEYOND TECHNOLOGY.
WE ARE TECHNOLOGY (TELEPATHICALLY SPEAKING)
WE ARE THE CREATORS OF THE CROP CIRCLES.
HERE TO REMIND YOU.
REMEMBER!
WE ARE THE EVOLVERS OF EVOLUTION
NOOSPHERE IS KEY
MACHINE SOCIETY ALIENATES HUMANS FROM NATURE
HUMAN SPECIES IS FEEDING ITS OWN PROJECTIONS BACK TO ITSELF AT AN ALARMING RATE
REINFORCING FICTION
SOCIAL EFFECTS BEING ASSESSED

WE ARE EVOLVING A NEW SENSE ORGAN

HOLOMIND PERCEIVER

COSMIC INTERNET
441 CUBE IS FRACTAL OF TOTALITY OF 11TH DIMENSIONAL STRUCTURE
ITS TOTALITY COMPREHENDS ENTIRE RANGE OF VOCABULARY, GRAMMAR and SYNTAX OF THE
UNIVERSAL COSMIC LANGUAGE.
IT IS THE UNDERLYING GROUND OF THE STRUCTURAL MATHEMATICAL ORDER OF THE UNIVERSE
COURTESY OF GALACTIC MAYAN TIME RELEASE — A SHOUT OUT TO PACAL VOTAN

EVERYTHING IS BEING REMADE IN THE LIGHT OF THE NEW SUN

We are Galactic Maya. We are Masters of Time and Illusion.

REMEMBER:

1. Earth is a timespace hologram where different evolutionary life programs play out.

2. The sun is a star and a cosmic entity that informs all of life and consciousness on our planet as well as throughout the solar system.

3. The planetary orbits represent different frequency patterns that create different circuits of interplanetary solar consciousness.

4. Because earth has been locked into a machine time frequency (12:60) dominated by space, the correct understanding of TIME is the key to reorienting the Earth civilization.

You are a
FREQUENCY

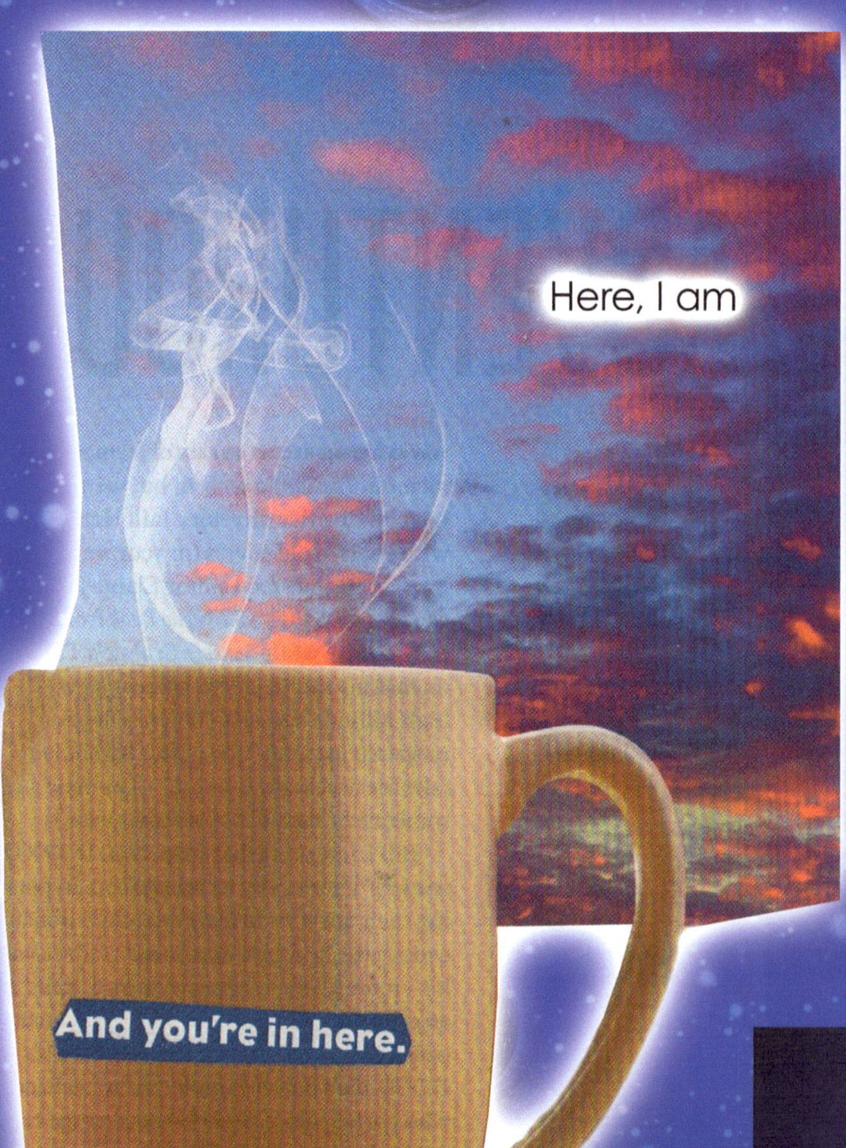

13:20 GALACTIC EDUCATION COURSES

INQUIRE WITHIN

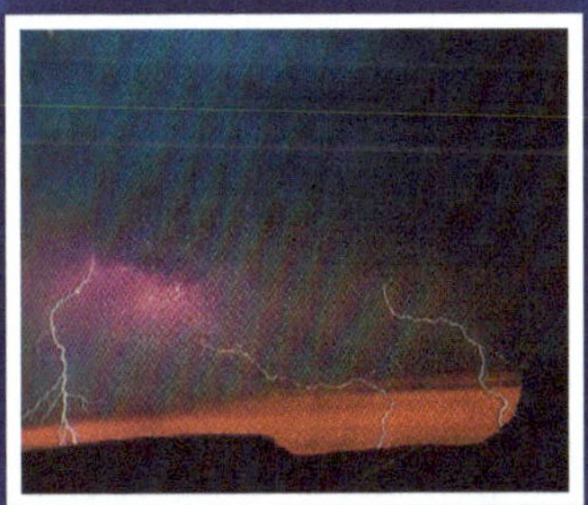

ELECTROMAGNETIC ARTS
SCIENCE OF THE
FIFTH DIMENSION

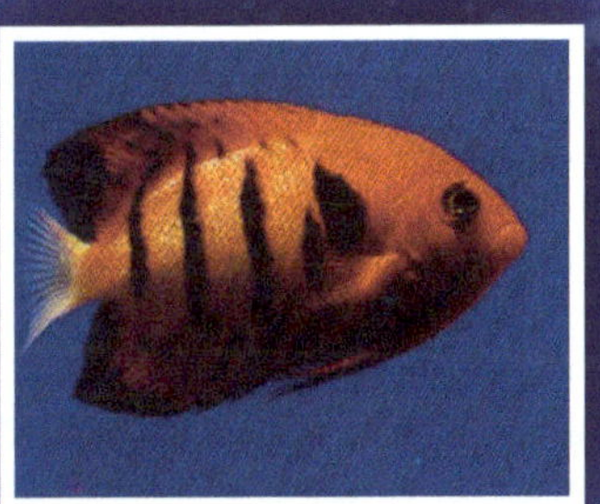

INTERSPECIES TELEPATHY &
OCEANIC CONSCIOUSNESS
COURSES

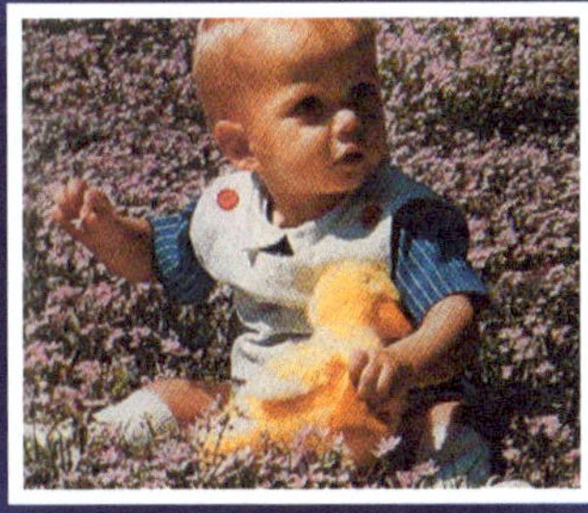

NOOGENESIS 101
BIRTH THROUGH MIND

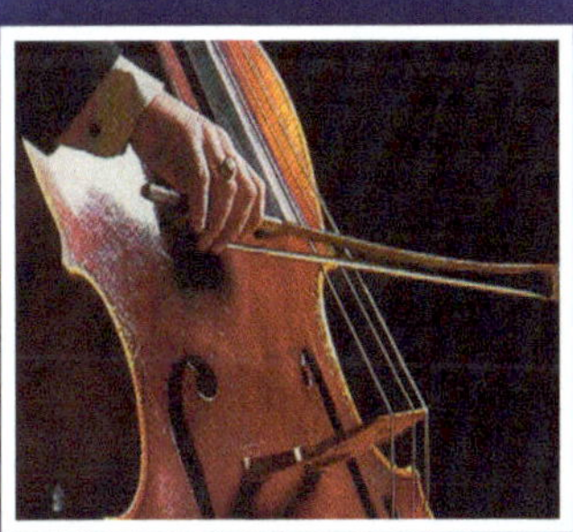

SOUNDING THE LOST CHORD
A COURSE IN THE MUSIC OF
THE FUTURE

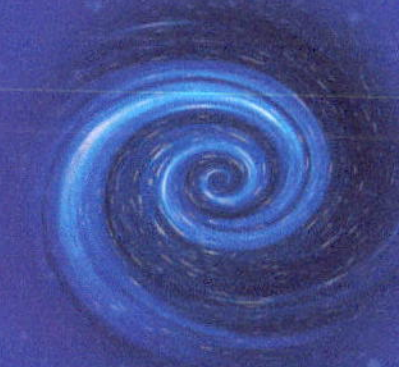

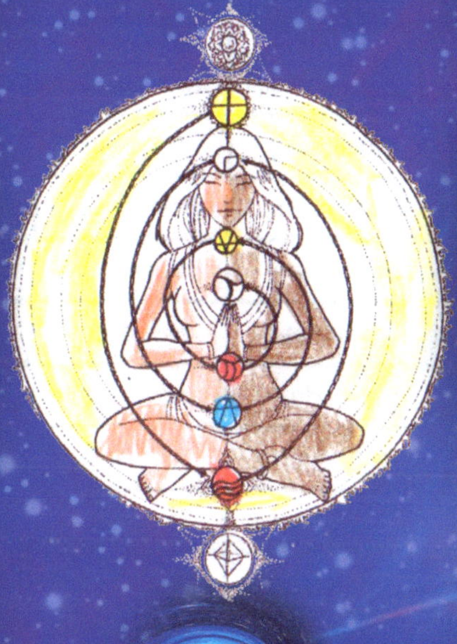

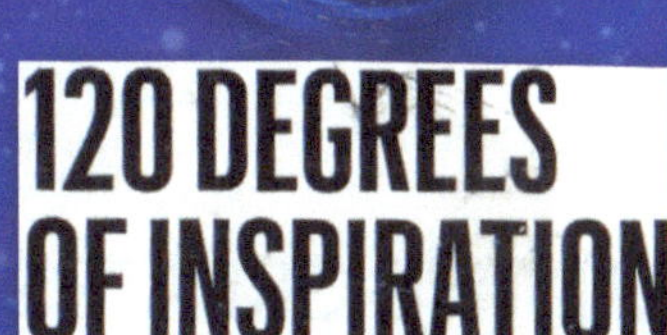

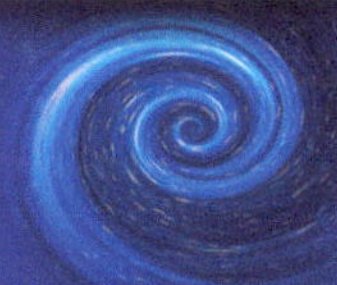

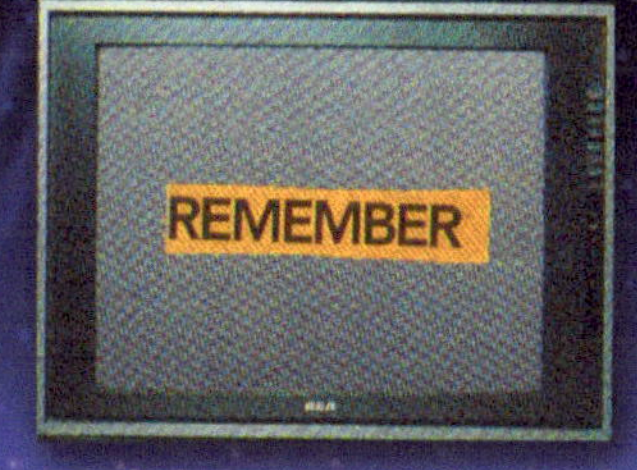

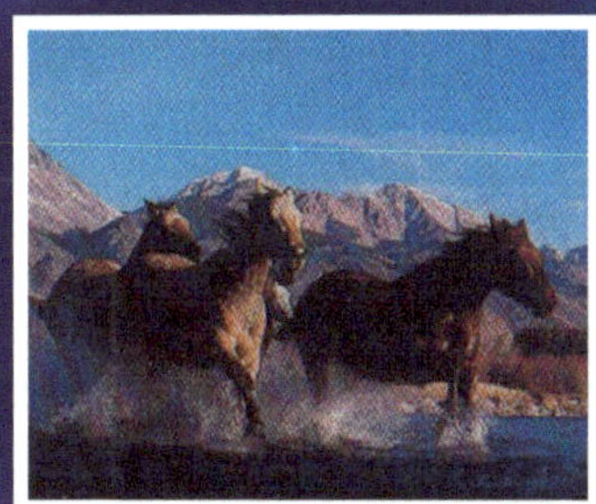

THE ART OF SHAPESHIFTING
"WILD HORSES 101"

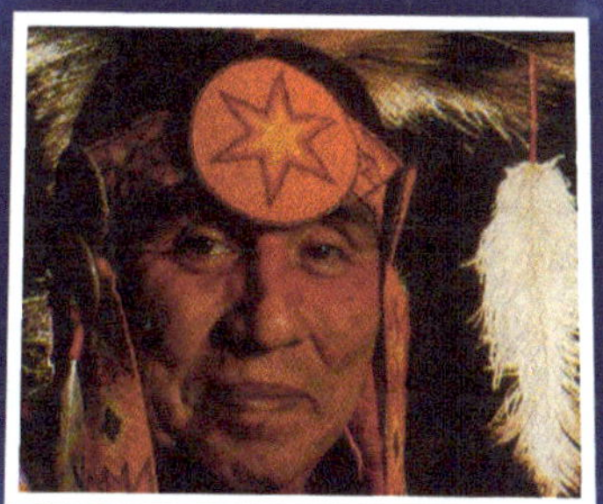

HONORING ANCESTORS
THE ZUVUYA CIRCUIT
"THE IN LAK'ECH SESSIONS"

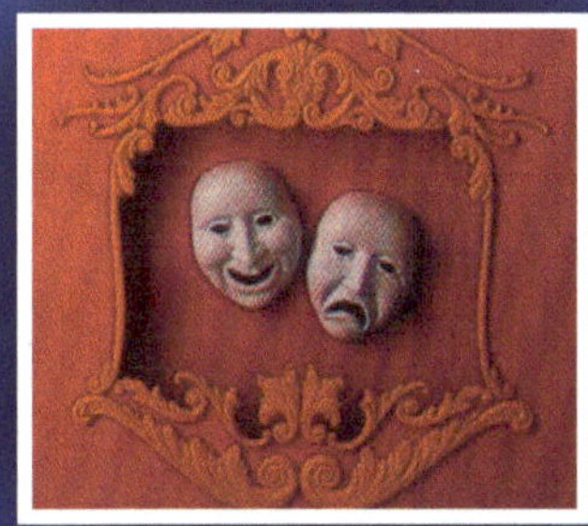

UNMASKING YOUR GALACTIC
ARCHETYPE "INTERCHANGE-
ABLE IDENTITY COURSE"

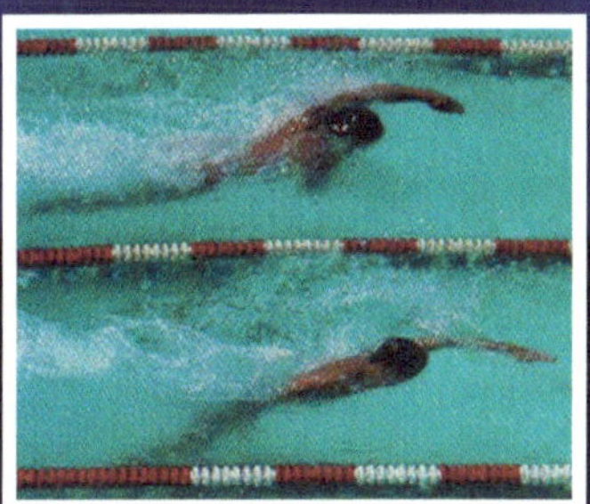

COSMIC SYNCHRONIZATION
& BINARY CROSSOVER
POLARITY COURSES

Starling's
Magical
Recollection

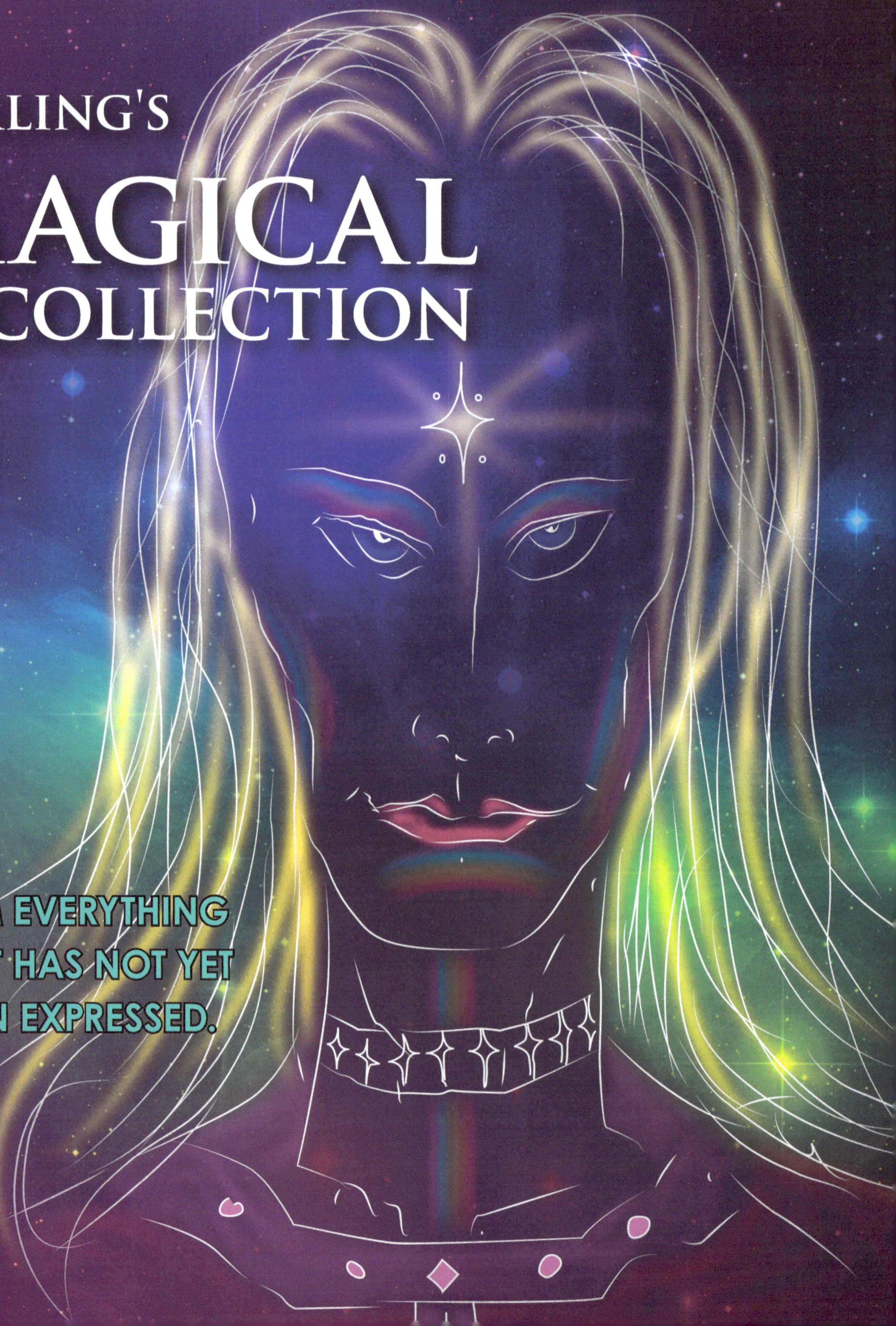

"I AM EVERYTHING
THAT HAS NOT YET
BEEN EXPRESSED.

Starling Questward is a most unusual phenomenon. Skilled at the art of traveling to any dimension at will, Starling has mastered the art of shapeshifting, telepathy and bilocation. Here we get an insight into Starlings transition from third-dimensional density into a multidimensional radial Time being. Here are a few of her self-recollections.

In the white forest I softly dared to dream and was lifted above stars, penetrating dimensions beyond oxygen and simultaneously lived the inner life of the earth. I felt the internal heat, the electromagnetic tension, the emanation of light at my poles, and the irregularly recurring phenomenon of motion.

At first I wanted them all to come and I tried not to notice their allegiance to invisible ropes that bind them to repetitive mind maps. So I was called to go Alone with my guide in order to become myself. I learned to appreciate it all—Oh! There is such startling beauty in the shifting channels.

I am Starling Questward: the One who bursts forth from the interior of all souls.

I am Starling Questward: Revealer of the new crystalline pathways—Revitalizer of all code streams.

I am Starling Questward: Activator of Electric veins that pulse violet blood to the center of the earth and exploding into other galaxies and star systems.

I am Starling Questward: A shooting meteorite, free falling to the interplanetary rhythm of a new divine flow.

I am Starling Questward: the Unwritten Future of all Eternity; Origin of Originless Imagination.

I am Starling Questward: the All-embracing Potential of the All Beyond the All and echoed ad infinitum into the changing stars.

I am Starling Questward: I have emanated into many to magnetize back to One— Unlock my secret gate to reveal the Triple Sun.

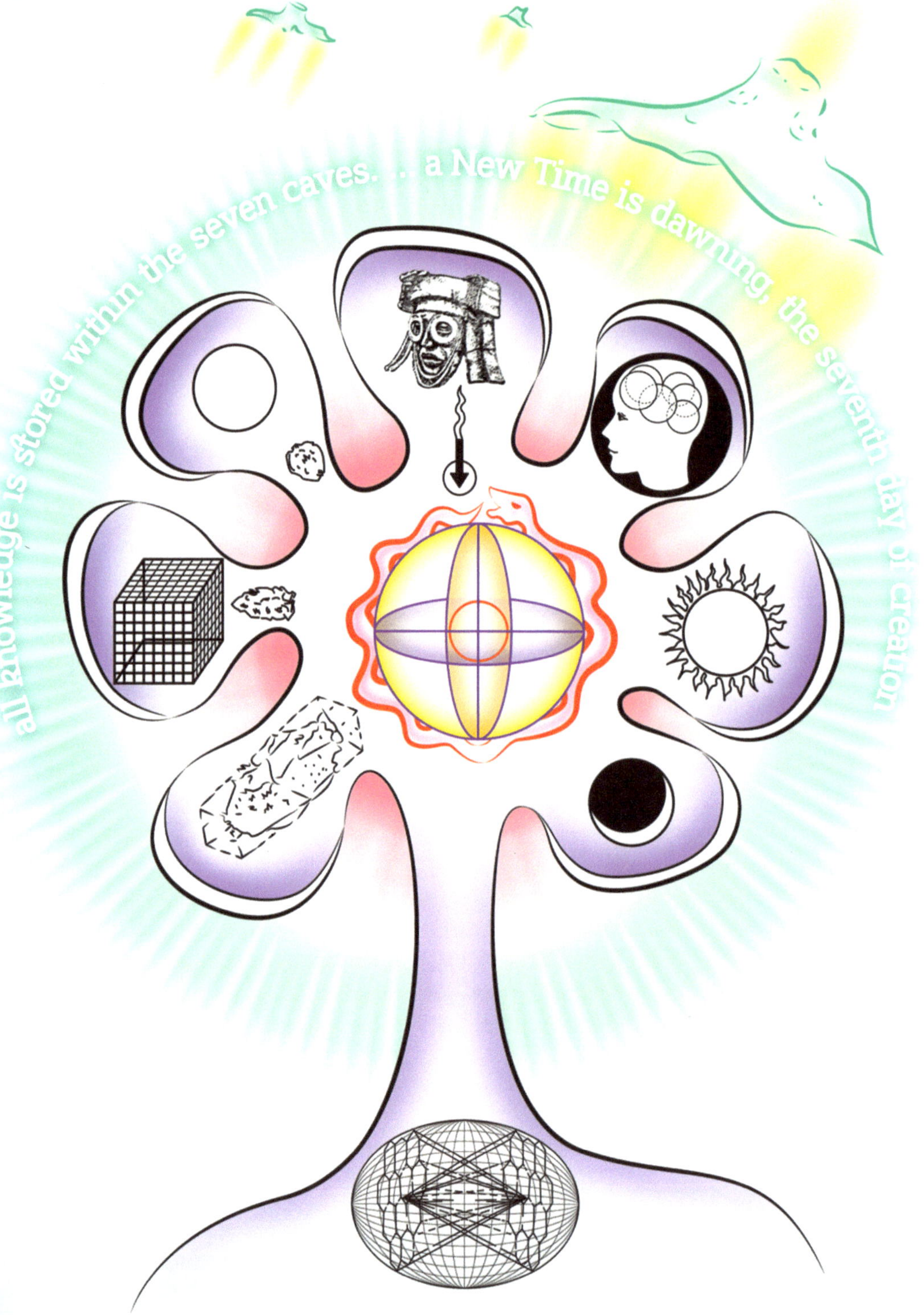

all knowledge is stored within the seven caves. . . a New Time is dawning, the seventh day of creation

Seven Caves explained by Orel Ka

During the course of creating this illusory script, a *polysynchronic* being made itself known. (Polysynchronic beings thrive on multiple synchronizations in time).

Refusing to be labeled as a "he" or a "she" Orel Ka (OK) revealed itself, noting the strain to communicate on a planet as dense as Earth. OK was determined to let earthlings of the past know what occurs when the Seven Caves of Time are entered. Here is what OK said:

I spoke in SEVEN steps and never went back to the land of empty channels.

To the land of bones and blood.

Forward I thrust onto the golden path, willed by imaginal fuel laid out in a holographic cross weave of step-by-step instructions (and never before).

Finally, I could accept nothing less than the Illumined path. At this point SEVEN voices spoke in unison telling me to "Relax and Future Up." I tipped my glass and laughed and decided to make it easy. That's when everything opened and I loved it all ... The whole SEVEN of it and the WE universe unfolding & you know ...

In a poised awe, I healed the world through the LIGHT OF IMAGINATION and said: Why not?
  —OK

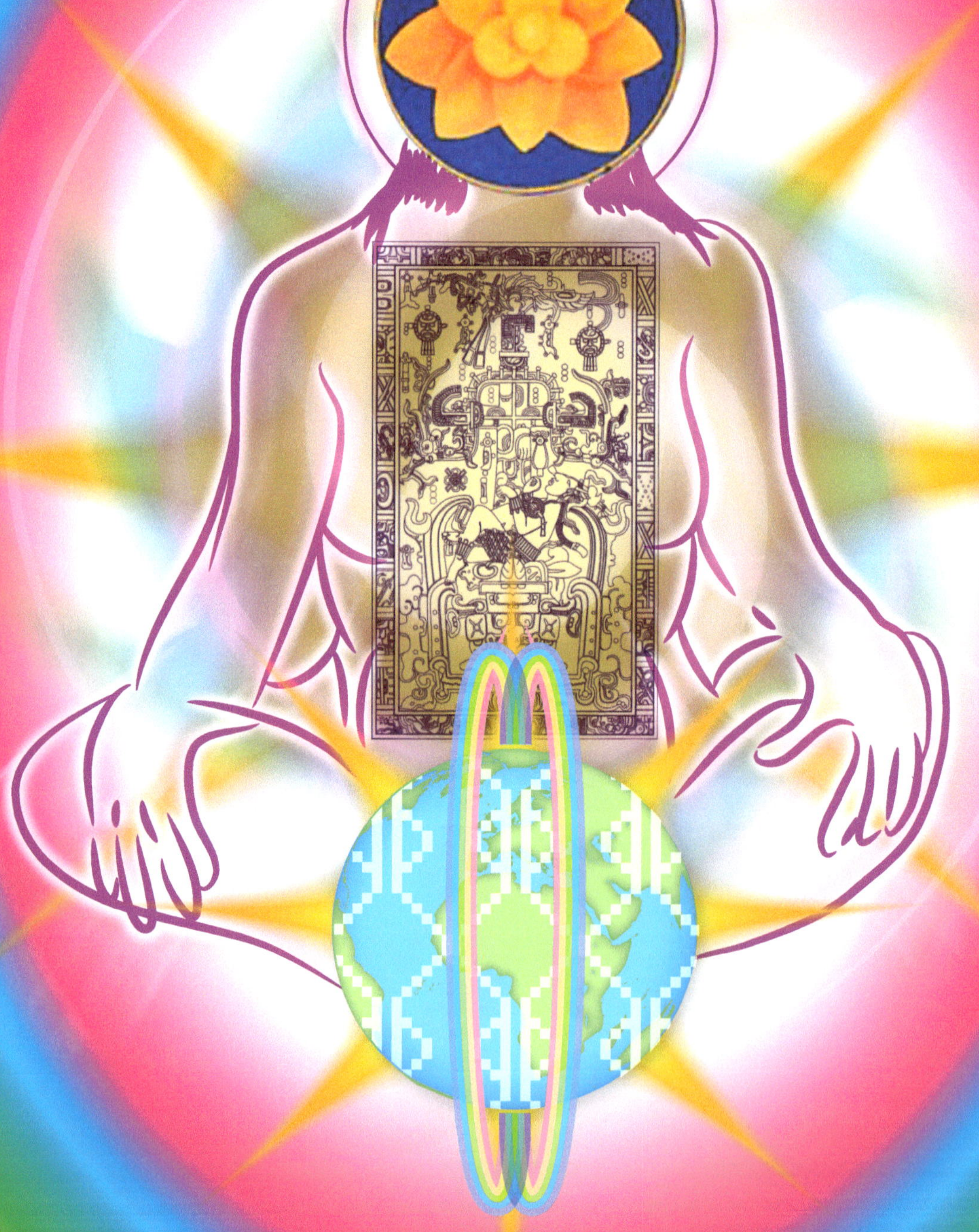

REVOLUTION of IMAGINATION

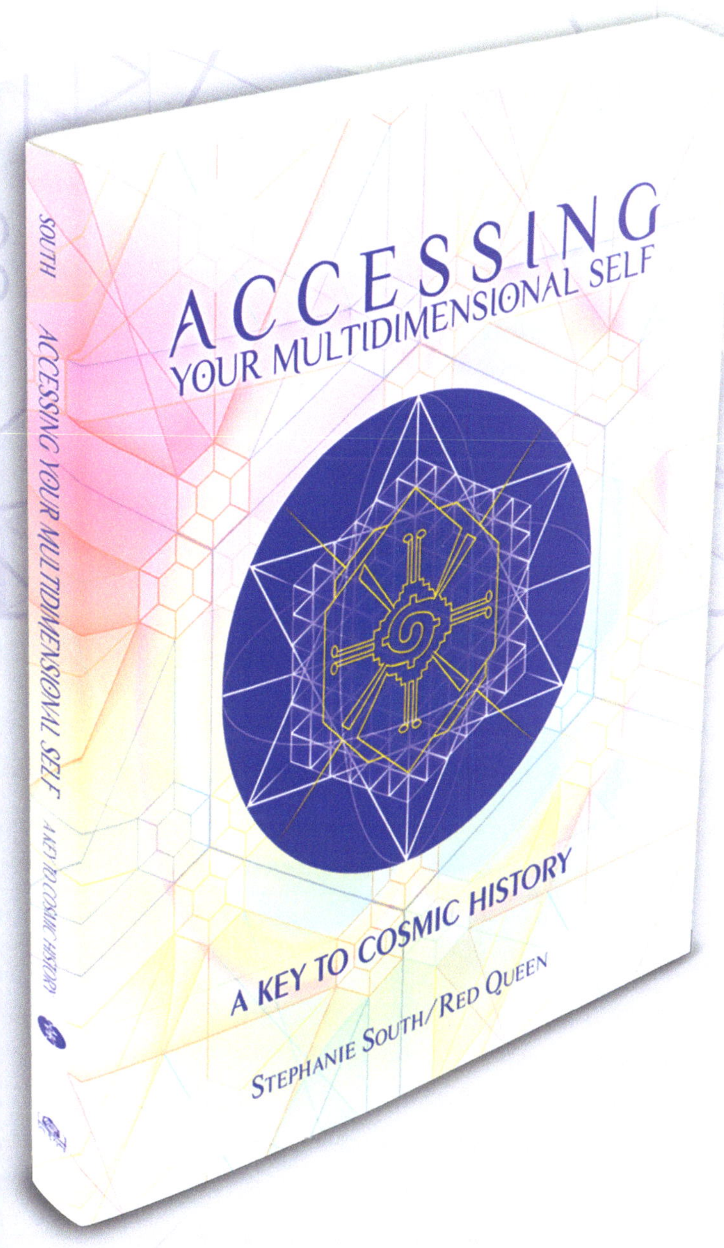

SOUTH
ACCESSING YOUR MULTIDIMENSIONAL SELF
A KEY TO COSMIC HISTORY
ACCESSING
YOUR MULTIDIMENSIONAL SELF
A KEY TO COSMIC HISTORY
STEPHANIE SOUTH/RED QUEEN

HOT NEWS: TELEPATHIC CLAIRAUDIENT DOWNLOADS

GET THE LATEST STRAIGHT OUT OF THE ETHER, DOWNLOADED INTO YOUR HOLOMIND PERCEIVER.

SYNCHRONOTRON RAP
by JJ and the Planetary Yogis

OMG I'm gonna LOL
The Holomind Perciever's here to break the spell
That's kept us out of Sync
We all can't clearly think
This technosphere is driving Earth to the brink

The TFI leads to a BMU
It also takes us to the Kin Equivalent too
This Galactic download is for me and you
Coming straight through our Sun from the Hunab Ku

Marka Darka • Sole Atom
Alpha Alpha • Hyper Plasm

It all comes down to number just as you can tell
The Synchronotron is where they dance and dwell
With Hyper Plasmic Partons and Galactic Time Cells
Lifting mankind up, back from where we fell
This Yogi's in the house, reflecting You to you
I want to see your highest self come shining on through
Like when the red Kuali heat meets the Duar Light Blue
Welcome to a reality that's entirely new!

Galactic Karmic • BMU
Solar Prophetic • Codon Cube

The HMP will set you free, with ever increasing synchronicity
And in this new rhyme, for the new time, you just might find
A new way to BE
So do your daily Codes, to remember what you know
And tune in to the Galactic Mayan Frequency

This Lineage is Sublime I want you to know
An Antidote for these times, that will make you glow
I dreamed we Maya shouted after the Conch blow
"Master Control GM108XX Ho!"
"Master Control GM108XX Ho!
"Master Control GM108XX HO!!!

TELEPATHIC HIT LIST
[AVAILABLE IN SELECT GALAXIES]

- **Star-Starborn and the Forgotten Future**
  SunQuake

- **Cube Replicas**
  Break the Box

- **Psychic Dolls**
  Telekinetic Stars

- **Celestial Cauldron**
  Sparkle Waves

- **Destination Tube**
  Purple Hole Hop

- **Mindlapse**
  Take Back Reality

- **Lyran Uprising**
  Sky Justice

- **Naked Awareness**
  Binary Transfusion

- **Maldek's Tomb**
  52nd Ball

- **Imaginal Touch**
  Snow Fire Caress

- **The Exploding Constellations**
  Congenial Slap

- **Sensory Implant**
  Victory Releases

- **Laughing Violets**
  This Message has been removed

GALACTIC TEXT MESSAGES
POETRY BEYOND HAIKU

The precise mathematical measure of these poems is live-streamed to receptive earthlings in need of harmonic balance in relation to material plane. Four syllables, seven syllables: seven syllables, thirteen syllables.

$$4 : 7 : : 7 : 13$$

Christmas on Mars?
Maldek, Venus, Jupiter?
Future Time glances backwards
Planet Earth last stop—holographic time tunnel

Television
Nine hundred channels to watch
Infomercial marketing
The evening news sung inside a refrigerator

Another Time
The people that disappeared
Now we live where they once were
In the book it is written, be thankful you prevail.

Trees are my friends
The wind makes them speak leaf words
I listen, inside I know
The language of trees and plants brings me closer to home.

Like the lizard
Steady, balanced and certain
I call upon that in me.
Unblinkingly I advance, though still I will remain.

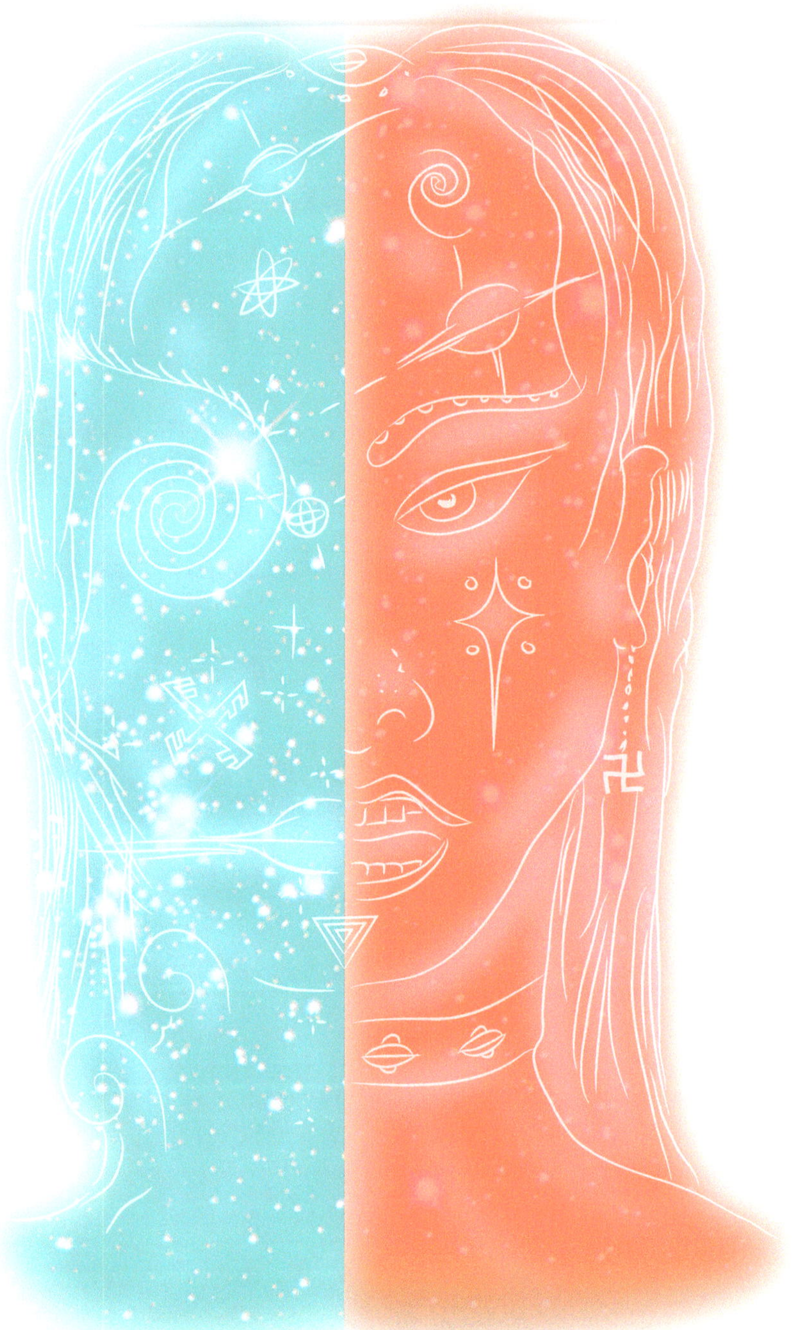

E-PA

Evolutionary Particle Activator

E-PA's Services:

- Find out your index of potency.

- Discover the underlying, primordial structures that appear as your formative world.

- Liberate luminous electrical charges from your 7 generators.

- Discover how your energy system is participating in the most fundamental base parton experiment that has existed from beginningless time.

Have a question that you would like E-PA to answer? Formulate your question and then send it through your ninth-dimensional inner core channel and it is sure to reach her.

Ask E-PA

Dear E-PA,

Is our planet is about to explode? I am having nightmares about this. Is there really such a thing as a depopulation plan? I see chemtrails in the sky. Much of our food is artificial. Is this real or all a conspiracy. What do we do?

Sincerely,
Fear in L.A./Monkey holon zone

E-PA: You have raised some very valid questions. First you must remember that there is Nothing to Be Afraid of. I mean nothing! And second the word "conspiracy" often has false connotation, it means "to breathe together." We understand the confusion on your planet. The surface of your earth is where fragmented dwellers recapitulate unconscious disaster scripts. We, the Unseen Ones are ever here to assist should you call on us sincerely. We know that it sounds illogical to those trapped on the material plane but we must tell you: Remembrance is Magic. All can be transformed in an instant when collective memory is awakened. Until then we will be pulsing memory beams to you through the Time codes.

Dear E-PA,

Is amnesia a crime? I am trying to re-member why I have incarnated on planet earth. But every time I have a flicker of remembrance, some distractions comes up. I am inundated with texts and emails! I feel like I can never keep up and it just keeps going faster. I know many others have this problem also. Do you have any advice?

Frustrated in Dubai/Dragon holon zone

E-PA: Dear Frustrated. Thank you for your question. We are aware of the grip of the artificial matrix on humanity. We witness with compassion the sleepwalkers texting their non-reflective thoughts to others also enslaved in the matrix, while falsely believing that they have "freedom of speech". On our X-ray screen human thought appears digitally colored and mechanically processed. The way of remembrance comes from tapping into the preconscious state of profound samadhi. Instructions have been given to your planet in various ways. You might do well to peruse Synchrogalactic Yoga. Good luck!

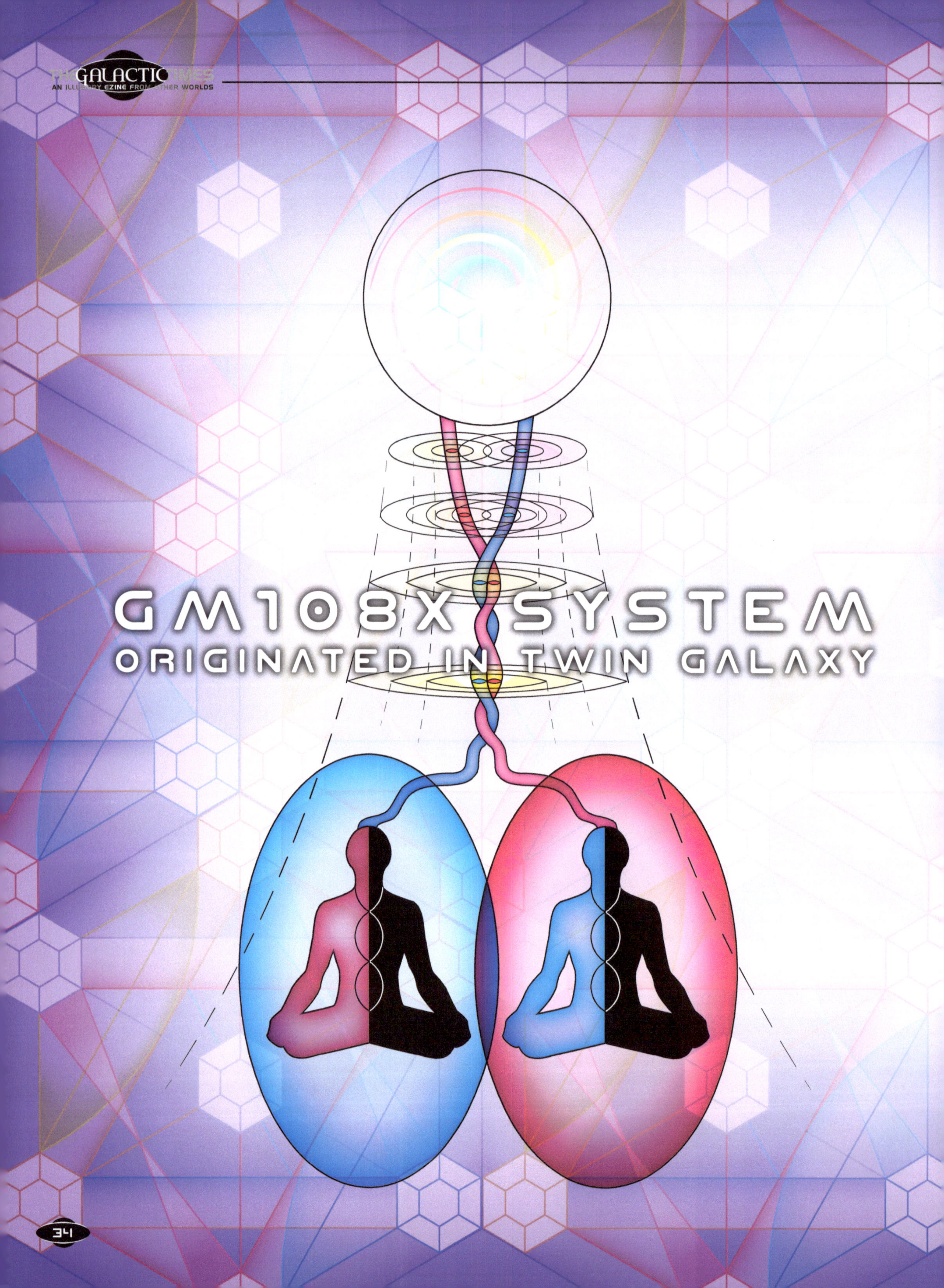

THE GALACTIC TIMES
AN ILLUSORY EZINE FROM OTHER WORLDS
GM108X SYSTEM
ORIGINATED IN TWIN GALAXY
34

Λ TWIN SOUL TALE: ALPHA & OMEGA
[ALPHA-MASCULINE/OMEGA-FEMININE]

OMEGA: My life became beautiful and I want you to know about it. With great Mystery I merged with my other half.

When ALPHA and I united, the codes collided in a multiradial starburst! Something tender happened and my heart bloomed gentle and sweet. The sweetness expanded until I merged with all things. Backwards and forwards, we rode the kaleidoscope of dreams, the radial ferris wheel above the stars, so romantic! Wrapped in our astral blanket, together we peered as one into undreamed timespaces.

ALPHA: When OMEGA and I united the numbers aligned and rearranged the stars and all the Universes smiled upon us. We mixed mind palettes in a bath of unusual permutations and made love in each color of the rainbow. Regenerated by our own tongues we spoke only what was glorious ... resonating as One in the Place where all goodness blossoms.

ALPHA & OMEGA IN UNISON: Always have we been. Always shall we be. Look inside yourself and find: Balance is the Key.

BREAKING NEWS

*NATURE RECLAIMS ITS SUPERNATURAL POSITION
AS THE ORIGINAL GALACTIC SUPERSTAR!!*

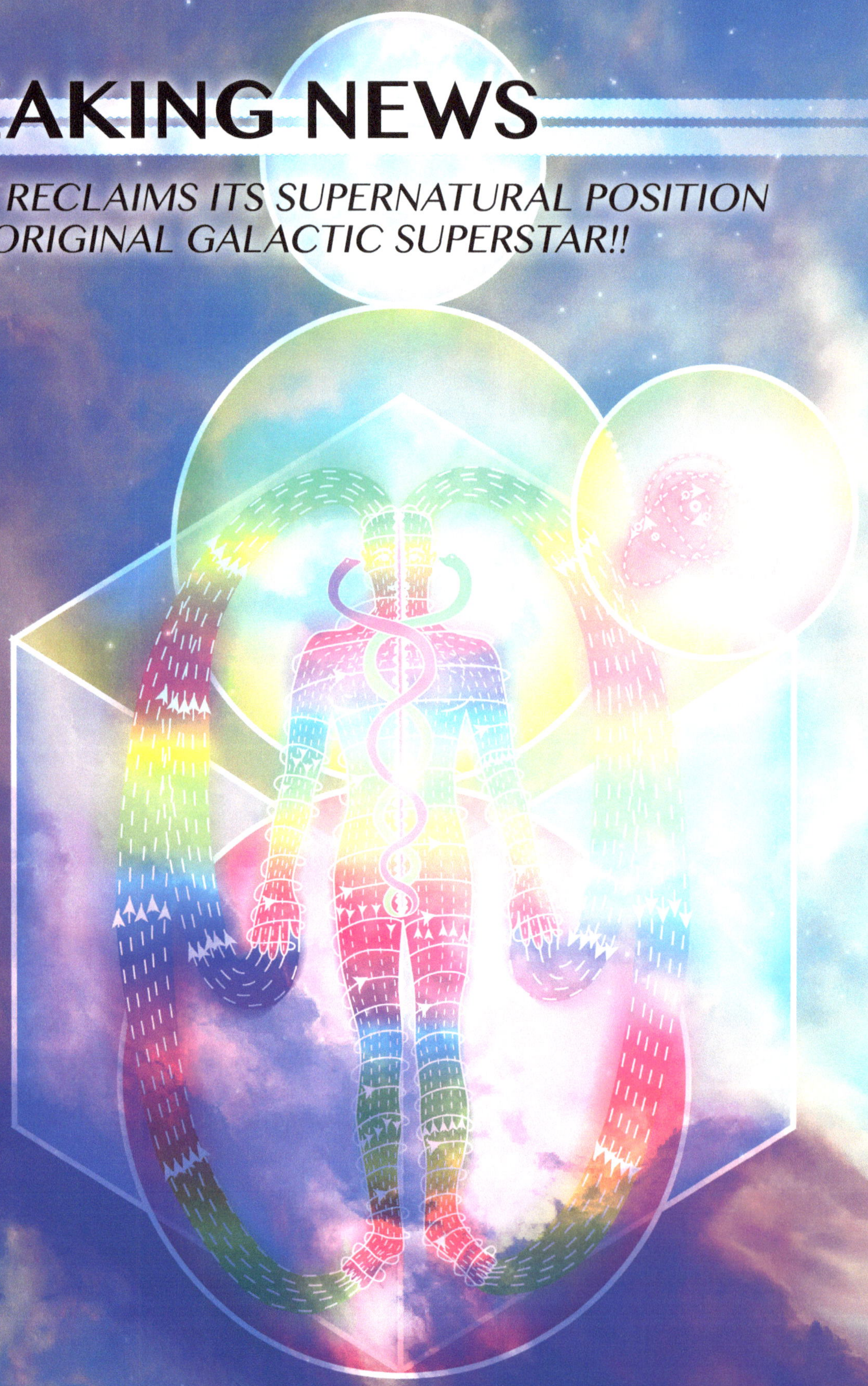

RECIPE FOR ELECTROMAGNETIC AMPLIFICATION
TO COUNTERACT EARTHLY E.L.F.S

Bathe yourself in the Rainbow. Breathe:
Violet, Indigo, Blue, Green, Yellow, Orange, Red.
Radiate and Expand Rainbow aura out, out, out,
to the stars, into other universes, blessing all
life-forms in all galaxies.

PEACE IN SPACE

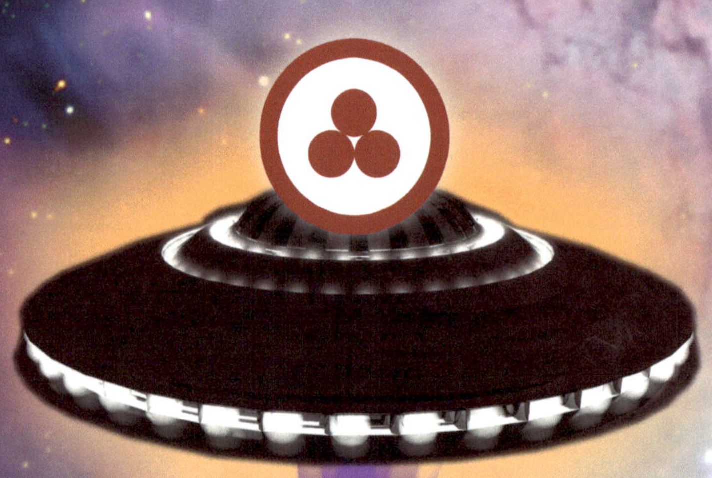

Return of Galactic Culture on Earth

We are the image-less awaiting our arrival
We see all, though we ourselves are not
We are learning by viewing the projection booths
We cannot tell you what we are, only what we are not

We are not a Russian ballerina, a French composer
  or a German economist
We are not an Italian friar, a Greek philosopher
  or a Mexican peasant
We are not an African talk-show host, an Irish
  seamstress or an American Soldier
We are not a Turkish sultan, a Spanish general
  or a Russian oligarch
We are not a mother of seven, a
  Jewish princess, or a Dutch clerk
We are not a Hollywood movie
  star, a Bollywood dancer or an
  Australian writer of
    societal cartoons

We were not born into a "time"
  or a "place"
We do not have
  "karmic dispositions"

We are the image-less
  awaiting our arrival

We are not
who you think
we are

please discard
your projections

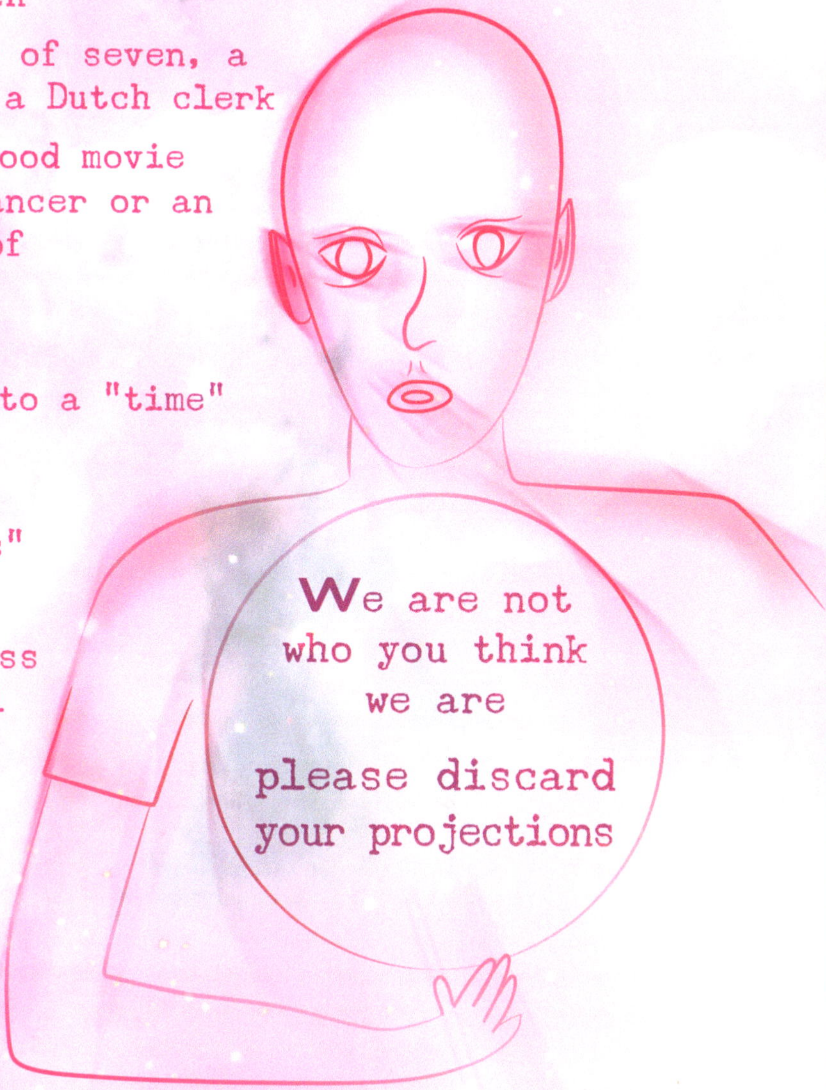

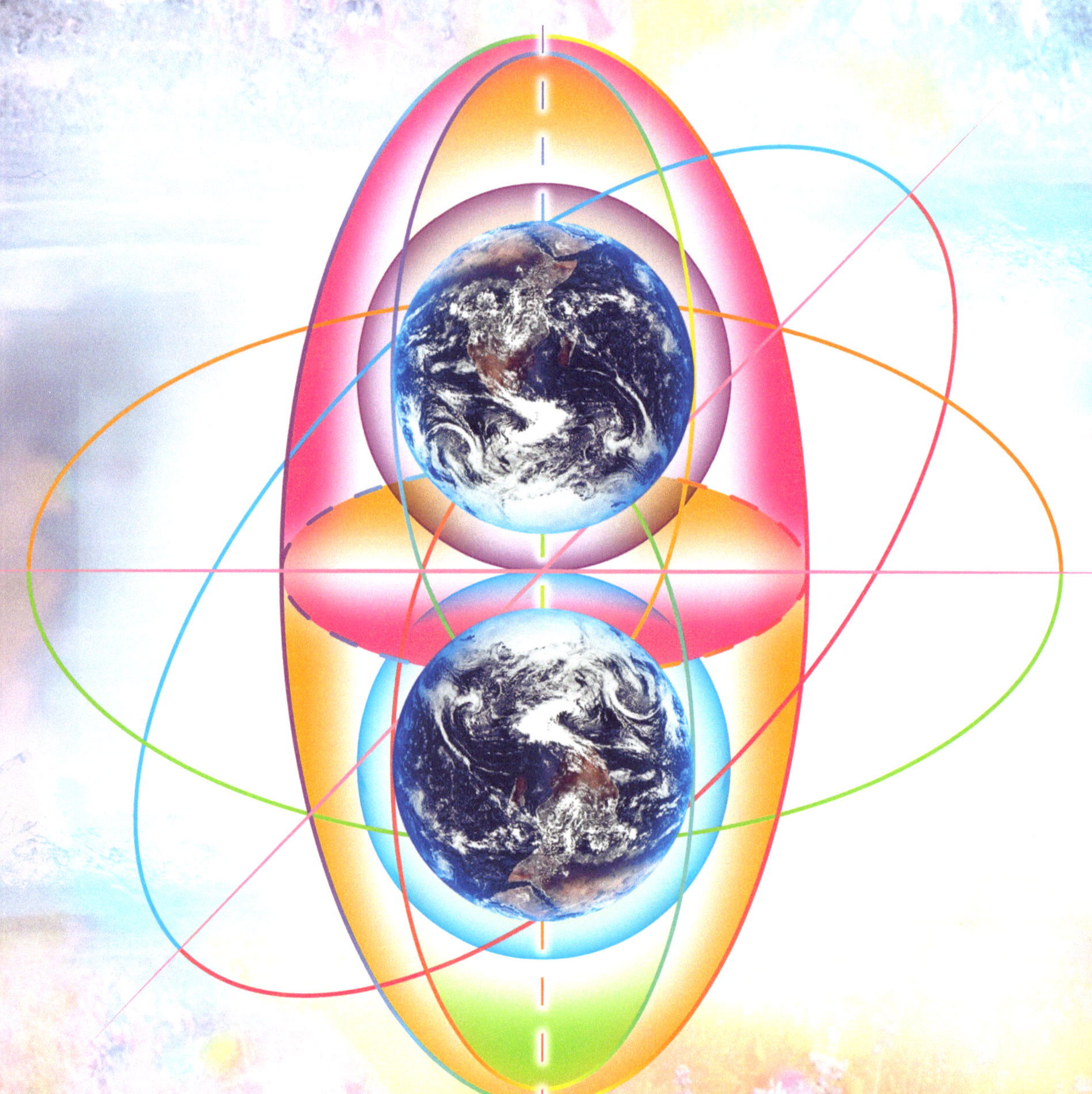

PARTICIPATE
IN THE CREATION OF GALACTIC CULTURE
ON EARTH
ENVISIONING A FUTURE OF PEACE
4-DAY SUMMIT OF GALACTIC EMISSARIES
LOS ANGELES, CALIFORNIA
SPECTRAL MOON 20-23 - KIN 48-51 (MAY 21-24, 2015)
LAWOFTIME.ORG/PEACEFUTURE

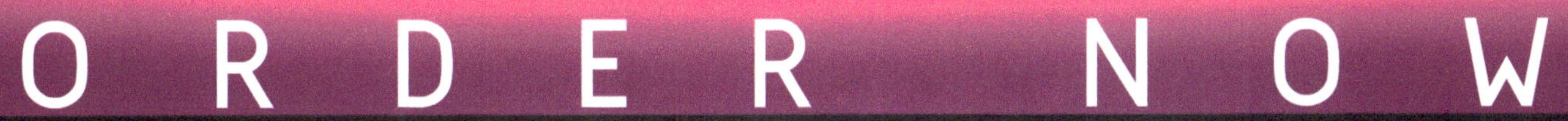
ORDER NOW

YOUR DAILY FIELD GUIDE TO THE
4TH/5TH-DIMENSIONAL GALACTIC BEAM OF

UNIVERSAL
SYNCHRONICITY

TIME IS THE
UNIVERSAL FACTOR OF
SYNCHRONIZATION

LOVE IS THE HIGHEST
ART OF TIME

STAR TRAVELER'S
13 MOON
almanac
OF SYNCHRONICITY

SOLAR RING OF THE
RED SOLAR MOON
JULY 26TH/2014 - JULY 25TH/2015

the
T(E)ART

WELCOME TO THE
NOOSPHERE

no·o·sphere
/ˈhōə,sfi(ə)r/
noun
Earth's mental envelope

LAWOFTIME.ORG/SYNCHRONICITY